CAMBRIDGE

Great Expectations
GCSE English Literature for AQA
Student Book

Jon Seal

Series editor: Peter Thomas

CAMBRIDGE
UNIVERSITY PRESS

University Printing House, Cambridge CB2 8BS, United Kingdom

Cambridge University Press is part of the University of Cambridge.

It furthers the University's mission by disseminating knowledge in the pursuit of
education, learning and research at the highest international levels of excellence.

www.cambridge.org
Information on this title: www.cambridge.org/9781107454125 (Paperback)
         www.cambridge.org/9781107454194 (Cambridge Elevate-enhanced Edition)
         www.cambridge.org/9781107454033 (Paperback + Cambridge Elevate-enhanced Edition)

© Cambridge University Press 2015

First published 2015

Printed in the United Kingdom by Latimer Trend

A catalogue record for this publication is available from the British Library

ISBN 978-1-107-45412-5 Paperback
ISBN 978-1-107-45419-4 Cambridge Elevate-enhanced Edition
ISBN 978-1-107-45403-3 Paperback + Cambridge Elevate-enhanced Edition

Additional resources for this publication at www.cambridge.org/ukschools

Cambridge University Press has no responsibility for the persistence or accuracy
of URLs for external or third-party internet websites referred to in this publication,
and does not guarantee that any content on such websites is, or will remain,
accurate or appropriate. Information regarding prices, travel timetables, and other
factual information given in this work is correct at the time of first printing but
Cambridge University Press does not guarantee the accuracy of such information
thereafter.

....

Message from AQA

This textbook has been approved by AQA for use with our qualification. This means that we have checked that it
broadly covers the specification and we are satisfied with the overall quality. Full details of our approval process can
be found on our website.

We approve textbooks because we know how important it is for teachers and students to have the right resources
to support their teaching and learning. However, the publisher is ultimately responsible for the editorial control and
quality of this book.

Please note that when teaching the GCSE English Literature (8702) course, you must refer to AQA's specification as
your definitive source of information. While this book has been written to match the specification, it cannot provide
complete coverage of every aspect of the course.

A wide range of other useful resources can be found on the relevant subject pages of our website: www.aqa.org.uk

Contents

Introduction

Welcome to your GCSE English Literature for AQA student book on *Great Expectations*. This is one of Dickens's best-known novels and we hope you will enjoy it first at GCSE and then later in life.

Much of the novel deals with subjects and problems you may be familiar with, including growing up, family, self-image and being in love. This book will help you get the most of the novel and do the best you can. It will develop your skills in reading and responding to a 19th-century novel and in writing for GCSE English Literature.

Part 1: Exploring the novel

Part 1 leads you through *Great Expectations*. It ensures you build a thorough understanding of the plot, structure and methods that Dickens used to create a popular and entertaining story for his magazine readers in 1860 – one that has maintained its popularity for 150 years. The units investigate the text, section by section, and provide activities for writing, drama and discussion that will deepen your experience, understanding, interpretations and analysis of the novel. Your work in each unit will provide you with notes and focused responses on aspects of the novel that are important to understand for GCSE.

Part 2: The novel as a whole

Part 2 provides an overview of key aspects of *Great Expectations*, including structure, characterisation and language. It will develop your detailed knowledge and understanding, as well as helping you revise your responses to the novel as a whole.

Preparing for your exam

The last part of this book gives you practice and guidance in preparing for your examination. It offers examples of answers showing skills at different levels so you can assess your own areas of strength and weakness, and focus your efforts to improve accordingly.

We hope that you will enjoy using this resource, not only to support your GCSE English Literature study but also to help you see that 19th-century novels have plenty to say about the life around you – and within you.

Peter Thomas
Series editor

Introducing *Great Expectations*

THE 19TH-CENTURY NOVEL AND *GREAT EXPECTATIONS*

The 19th-century novel

Dickens wrote in an age long before television and digital media. Cheap printing made books and magazines available to increasing numbers of people. Dickens made a living out of writing novels, but he was not the first to do so. Before him, Jane Austen and Walter Scott had built a loyal readership of their published fiction. William Thackeray – only seven months older than Dickens – was also releasing stories in magazine instalments before publishing them as single-volume novels.

In the 1850s and 1860s, these weekly or monthly magazines were a major source of entertainment. They offered a mixture of news features, articles on crime and accounts of travels. The serial story was a major selling point – readers would queue up to buy the latest instalment, keen to find out how the previous issue's cliff-hanger was resolved.

Dickens the writer

Charles Dickens was born in 1812 and died in 1870. He is one of the greatest writers of the Victorian period and wrote some of the best-loved novels of all time. Dickens never went to university and even his schooling was interrupted. As a boy he worked in a factory, and he went on to be a journalist before trying his hand at writing stories.

For most of his life, Dickens made his living by writing to entertain adults. He wrote for his own magazines, first *Household Words* then *All the Year Round*, both of which offered a mixture of social comment and fiction. As his reputation grew, he built on his success by producing stories designed to appeal to everyone, throwing into the mix elements of romance, humour, mystery, crime and the less glamorous side of life in Britain's great capital, London.

Dickens wrote about 16 novels all together (depending on what you count as a novel), as well as short stories and articles. His books were so successful that he became very wealthy, and he further increased his income by touring the UK and the USA giving readings from his novels. *Great Expectations* was written and published in 1860–61, but the novel is set earlier in the century – in the period of Dickens's own childhood and youth.

Structure and plot

Great Expectations is divided into three parts:

* Pip's early life and the discovery that he has been left some money
* the time he spends in London learning how to be a gentleman
* learning about his benefactor and his eventual return to the scene of his childhood.

 Find out more about structure and plot in the novel in Unit 11.

Pip's progress in the novel is a journey that begins and ends at Joe Gargery's forge. This gives the novel a circular structure that reflects one of Dickens's key themes – the development of a young man who goes on a journey of discovery, finally understanding what should be most valued in life.

Context and setting

The immediate context of the novel is England in the early to mid-19th century, with scenes set amongst the marshes of the Thames estuary and in London. The novel offers a window into Dickens's times, including information about the legal system and life in London. Dickens also draws on his knowledge of seafaring and trade on the Thames (his father worked in the shipping trade) to provide a backdrop to parts of *Great Expectations*.

 Find out more about context and setting in the novel in Unit 12.

The wider context is of 19th-century fiction being used not only to entertain the magazine-buying public, but also to give a realistic insight into the types of people and the institutions that made up society in Dickens's time. This novel is packed with details about trades and professions, and filled with observations of people in both their private lives and public roles.

Characterisation

Characters from every walk of life inhabit the novel and Dickens shows great skill in making them all believable. He does this by focusing on details of their appearance, their movements and speech habits, as well as what they actually say and do.

 Find out more about character and characterisation in the novel in Unit 13.

Ideas

Dickens was much concerned with the injustices he saw in the world around him. He shows great sympathy for the poor in 19th-century society, and he empathises with the harshness that many children experienced in their homes and schools. He is particularly good on how people manage to keep their dreams and fantasies alive in the face of difficulties and drawbacks, and how events often influence the development of someone's personality.

 Find out more about themes and ideas in the novel in Unit 14.

Interpretation

Your own response to the novel matters. What you think of the characters, which parts of the novel make you think or smile, which sections relate to your own experience – all these things will help you write about *Great Expectations* in an interesting way. Most important is what the novel means to you when it shows you ways that people behave, and how relationships develop or go wrong.

Language

Dickens uses narrative text and dialogue with equal skill. His narrative helps to convey realistic impressions of places and people, designed to evoke different emotions in the reader – amusement or sadness, perhaps. The description of Jaggers biting his crooked finger, for example, builds a memorable picture of this character. So too does his description of Wemmick's mouth, which is relaxed at home but becomes rigid and lacking in expression at work:

Wemmick was at his desk, lunching – and crunching – on a dry hard biscuit; pieces of which he threw from time to time into his slit of a mouth, as if he were posting them.

By degrees, Wemmick got dryer and harder as we went along, and his mouth tightened into a post-office again.

Dialogue allows Dickens to give his characters individual speech habits that also helps to build a picture of their personality – for example Joe's fondness for the word 'Ram-page' and Pumblechook's long-winded, pompous sentences. A character's language often also reflects their position in society and their circumstances at a given moment in the story. For example Magwitch's speech at the beginning of the novel suggests both his low social status and the urgency of his current situation, as well as his intention to frighten Pip:

'You get me a file.' He tilted me again. 'And you get me wittles.' He tilted me again. 'You bring 'em both to me.' He tilted me again. 'Or I'll have your heart and liver out.' He tilted me again.

 Find out more about language in the novel in Unit 15.

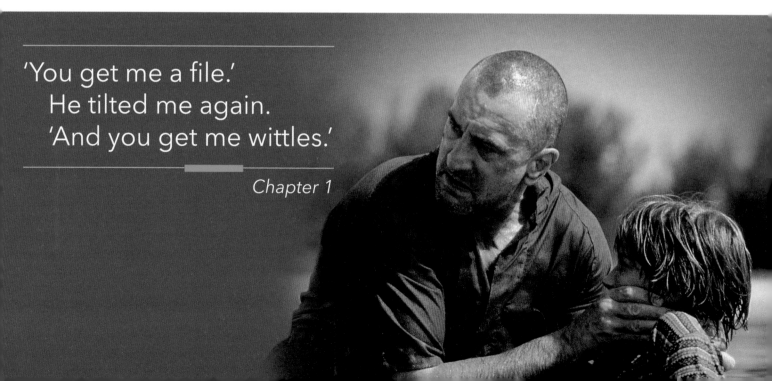

'You get me a file.'
He tilted me again.
'And you get me wittles.'

Chapter 1

THE 19TH-CENTURY NOVEL AND GCSE ENGLISH LITERATURE

Your GCSE English Literature course has been designed to include a range of drama, prose and poetry. *Great Expectations* will probably be one of the longer texts you will study, but it is a great story, filled with interesting and amusing characters, mysteries and plot twists.

At the end of your GCSE course in English Literature you will sit an exam. This is made up of two papers:

- **Paper 1: Shakespeare and the 19th-century novel**. This is worth 40% of your GCSE English Literature.
- **Paper 2: Modern texts and poetry**. This is worth 60% of your GCSE English Literature.

In Paper 1, there are two sections:

- **Section A: Shakespeare**. You will answer one question on the play you have studied. You will be required to write in detail about an extract from the play and then to write about the play as a whole.
- **Section B: The 19th-century novel**. You will answer one question on the novel you have studied – *Great Expectations*. You will be required to write in detail about an extract from the novel and then to write about the novel as a whole.

GCSE ENGLISH LITERATURE ASSESSMENT OBJECTIVES

The assessment objectives form the basis for the GCSE English Literature mark scheme. Your answer in Paper 1, Section B (the 19th-century novel) will be read by an examiner who will be guided by these three assessment objectives, as follows:

AO1: Read, understand and respond to texts. Students should be able to:

- maintain a critical style and develop an informed personal response
- use textual references, including quotations, to support and illustrate interpretations.

AO2: Analyse the language, form and structure used by a writer to create meanings and effects, using relevant subject terminology where appropriate.

AO3: Show understanding of the relationships between texts and the contexts in which they were written.

 Learning checkpoint

The assessment objectives mean that in your GCSE English Literature exams you need to show that you:
✔ understand what has been written
✔ have formed opinions about the book and are able to express them
✔ understand how the language makes things seem real, interesting, amusing or frightening; you have something to say about the form the writing takes and how it is structured
✔ have some sense of context for the events in the book, the time it was written and how it may be relevant today
✔ can support your arguments and opinions by quoting from the novel.

LITERATURE SKILLS AND STUDY FOCUS AREAS

During your course of study you will develop the core skills to show understanding, interpretation and analysis. These, along with the following study areas, give a focus for your work in this book.

Ideas, attitudes and feelings

You will be expected to understand and respond to the feelings, ideas or attitudes expressed in the novel. These three things all relate to **content**:

- **Ideas** are the thoughts that explain or result from an experience.
- **Attitudes** are the positions or postures adopted when facing experiences.
- **Feelings** are the emotions people experience, which are often quite different from their attitudes and ideas.

For example you could say that:

- an **idea** is that having great expectations of life **can lead people to believe** they are better than others
- an **attitude** is that Trabb's boy **should respect** someone who is successful in life
- a **feeling** is **frustration** that Trabb's boy makes such a public mockery of someone who is his superior.

The writer's methods

You will also be expected to understand and respond to the way in which the novel is written – the writer's methods. These amount to language, form and structure. Again, these are three distinct things. In the case of *Great Expectations*, for example, you could say that:

- the **language** of speech shows something about the class and education of the speaker
- the **form** is a serialised novel narrated by a main character
- the **structure** is based on Pip's development as he grows up and is influenced by various conditions and people.

Written response skills

Skill levels at GCSE English Literature can be simplified into three broad categories: understanding, explaining and conceptualising. This book will help you identify your current skill level and show you how to improve.

In each unit, you will find examples to help you develop your responses to the novel. They show how you can develop from basic comments (those that are relevant and include a supporting quotation) to using your skills in understanding and interpretation to explain feelings, motives or reasons and to include ideas that develop and extend meaning. The following are examples of each type of response.

Understanding

'Great Expectations' is about what happens when Pip, a small boy 'a bundle of shivers' meets an escaped convict and helps him by getting him some 'wittles' and a file. Although the convict gets caught, he always remembers the kindness of the boy, and decides to leave him some money, which lets him face life with 'great expectations'.

Explaining

It is about a young blacksmith's apprentice, Philip 'Pip' Pirrip, who is left some money by a mysterious benefactor in order for him to become a gentleman. He doesn't realise that the benefactor is the escaped convict he once helped, but wrongly thinks it must be a rich local woman Miss Havisham. Dickens shows his progress as he follows his 'great expectations', leaving his humble life in the marshes behind him and making new friends in London. He becomes more and more snobbish, until he finds out who has been helping him all along.

Conceptualising

Dickens uses Pip's progress from a 'small bundle of shivers' on the estuary marshes to a wealthy young man-about-town in London to show the effects of wealth and society on character. Mixing with rich, upper-class people such as Bentley Drummle and the Finches of the Grove makes him look down on the village forge where he grew up, and embarrassed by the people who live there. Dickens relates how Pip finally learns that his wealth comes from the escaped convict whom he helped when he was a child, and how this is a turning point as he begins to value the people and the human qualities that really matter in life.

Writing with focus

Each unit helps you develop focused writing skills, so you can be confident about writing in timed conditions in your exam. Be prepared to show how Dickens builds Pip's character and uses other characters to provide humour and insight into work, dreams and life – all of which are part of the novel's rich depiction of life in England in the mid-19th century. Your responses should make your points quickly, link to specific details from the text and show a clear purpose.

DICKENS AND YOU

We hope your lasting memory of the novel is of comical moments such as Joe's use of gravy to make Pip feel better, Trabb's boy's mockery of Pip as a snobbish returnee to the village, Wemmick's pride in his Walworth home as a castle and his crafty courtship of Miss Skiffins. We also hope that you will remember moving scenes such as Miss Havisham's preserved wedding items, Joe's embarrassment and awe at meeting Pip in London, and the dramatic and emotional ending, including Magwitch's fate. Finally, we hope that you enjoy reading the whole novel because of its constantly changing pace and variety, as well as its mixture of scenes, events and people.

1

Setting up prospects and problems

How does Dickens introduce his characters and setting?

Your progress in this unit:

- explain how Dickens establishes characters and setting at the start of the novel
- explore the link between characters and setting
- write the opening to your own story with a distinct setting
- understand a literature writing task
- create your own key extract from the opening of the novel.

GETTING STARTED – THE STORY AND YOU

Setting and story

The following speaking and listening activity will help you explore some ideas that you will later build into a story of your own.

1 Work in pairs. Think of the loneliest place you have ever been, for example an empty street, a dark woodland or a deserted beach. Describe it in detail to your partner. When you have finished your description, your partner should ask questions to try and find out more detail. Afterwards, swap over so you are the one asking the questions.

2 Repeat Activity 1, describing different types of **setting**. You might try and describe a desert, a night-time park in a large city or a marsh.

 Watch two actors try this activity on Cambridge Elevate.

Setting and character

The setting for a story should not only be an interesting place, it should also be linked to character and plot. The **characters** in a good story are part of the landscape.

1 Work in pairs. One of you should choose a setting and describe it briefly. The other then describes a character to put in that setting, explaining why the character is there. For example they might live there or work there, they may have been born there or they could be there to attack the place.

You can use one of the settings you described before or choose a new one – perhaps a multi-storey car park or a graveyard.

 Watch writers discussing their ideas on Cambridge Elevate.

GETTING CLOSER – FOCUS ON DETAILS

How does Dickens use the early chapters to draw his readers into the story?

Read through the key details and quotations from Chapters 1–7 to get an overview of the section you are about to explore.

Chapter 1

Pip, a young orphan boy, is visiting the graves of his family on Christmas Eve. He encounters a convict whose legs are shackled in irons.

'Blacksmith, eh?' said he. And looked down at his leg.

Chapter 2

Pip thinks about stealing some food and drink from his sister, Mrs Joe Gargery – with whom he lives – for the convict.

My sister … had brought me up 'by hand.'

Chapter 3

The following morning he returns to the marshes with brandy, a pie and a file for the convict.

The last I heard of him, I stopped in the mist to listen, and the file was still going.

Chapter 4

At Christmas dinner, Uncle Pumblechook drinks the brandy that Pip has diluted with tar water. Pip is afraid that they will also discover the missing pie and accuse him.

But, I ran no further than the house door, for there I ran head foremost into a party of soldiers with their muskets.

Chapter 5

Pip and his sister's kindly husband, Joe, accompany the soldiers in their search for the convict. He is caught and says he stole the pie.

Chapter 6

Pip feels guilty.

Chapter 7

Pip reads to Joe.

Key terms

setting: the description of the place in which a novel is set.

characters: the people in a story; even when based on real people, characters in novels are invented or fictionalised.

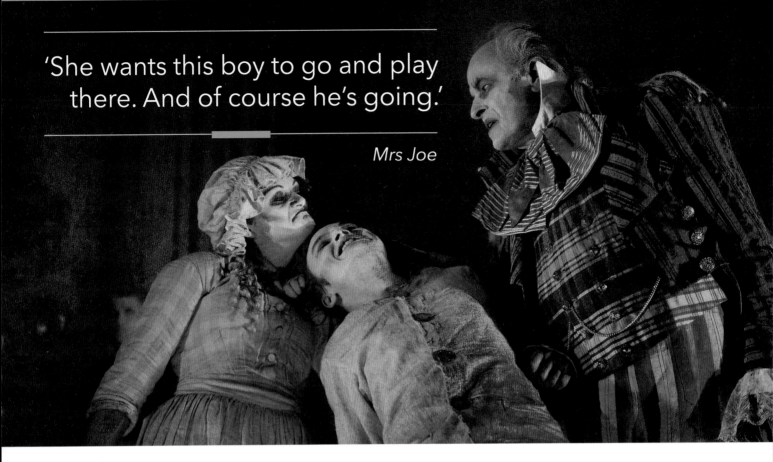

'She wants this boy to go and play there. And of course he's going.'

Mrs Joe

1 The quotations to accompany the summaries of Chapters 5, 6 and 7 are missing from the chart. Which of the following quotations goes with which chapter?

a 'Is there any Miss Havisham down town?' returned my sister. 'She wants this boy to go and play there. And of course he's going.'

b 'I wish to say something respecting this escape. It may prevent some persons laying under suspicion alonger me.'

c In a word, I was too cowardly to do what I knew to be right, as I had been too cowardly to avoid doing what I knew to be wrong.

 Watch characters introduce the story on Cambridge Elevate.

 Watch the characters summarise the story so far on Cambridge Elevate.

Linking character and setting

In the first two pages of the book, Dickens introduces two important characters and describes the setting. He also shows **links** between the characters and the setting. He sets the scene with a description of the marshland landscape:

… the dark flat wilderness beyond the churchyard, intersected with dykes and mounds and gates, with scattered cattle feeding on it, was the marshes; and that the low leaden line beyond, was the river; and that the distant savage lair from which the wind was rushing was the sea … .

A convict then emerges from this threatening setting. The words '**hold your noise**' are the first speech in the book. Up to this point we have heard the voice of the young narrator, Pip, talking about himself. We have learnt that he is an orphan and seen him visit the graves of his parents and siblings. Quite a lot of this information is written in an amusing way. Then suddenly a man jumps out and grabs him.

1 This is a particularly cinematic moment, and in film adaptations of *Great Expectations*, directors often make the most of it. David Lean's film version was one of the first, made in 1946. Look at the still image from the film.

a List any differences between this film image and the way you imagined the opening of the **novel** when you read it.

b How does this film image create an atmosphere of menace? How does the novel use language to do so in the first two pages?

c Write down four bullet points explaining how terrifying this is for Pip. For example:

- *He is all alone in a churchyard.*
- *He …*

Key terms

novel: a long story written in prose, describing characters and events.

Contexts

According to the 1861 census, 75% of males and 65% of females could read and write, but the literacy level of many of these people would have been very low. Despite this, Dickens was enjoyed by people in all sections of society and with different levels of education, so how did he achieve this popularity?

Great Expectations first appeared in the monthly magazine *All Year Round*, which had a readership of about 100,000. This opened it up to people on modest incomes, who could find small amounts of money regularly, so it was not only the prosperous ruling class who had access to Dickens's works, but also those with office jobs and some skilled people who worked with tools. In addition, people who were literate often read to those who were not. One illiterate cleaner surprised her employer by showing she knew about Dickens's novel *Dombey and Son*:

It turned out that she lodged at a snuff-shop kept by a person named Douglas, where there were several other lodgers; and that on the first Monday of every month there was a Tea, and the landlord read the month's number [episode] of *Dombey*, those only of the lodgers who subscribed to the tea partaking of that luxury, but all having the benefit of the reading.

PUTTING DETAILS TO USE

Setting and character

Use the following tasks to investigate the opening chapters more closely. Make notes of your answers. You will need these for the writing activity later in this unit.

1 The opening sentence of the book names the **narrator** as Philip Pirrip, but adds that his nickname is 'Pip'. Why do you think Dickens chose to call his character Pip?

   a Write down five bullet points summarising Pip's situation at the start of the novel. Mention who has died and who takes care of him.

   b Write down three quotations from the start of the novel that seem to emphasise Pip's loneliness. Whom has he never met, for example?

   c Find three clues in Chapter 1 that suggest the writer is an older man looking back. Consider the language he uses.

Key terms

narrator: the character in a novel who tells the story in the first person.

Later, in Chapter 2, we learn a bit more about Pip's situation:

> My sister, Mrs Joe Gargery, was more than twenty years older than I, and had established a great reputation with herself and the neighbours because she had brought me up 'by hand.'

As a child, Pip had not understood the expression 'by hand' and adds that his sister had:

> … a hard and heavy hand, and to be much in the habit of laying it upon her husband as well as upon me.

2 a What do you think Mrs Joe means when she says '**by hand**'?

   b Write two or three sentences about the relationship between Mrs Joe and her husband, Joe Gargery. Be careful to distinguish between what you know (because Chapter 2 says so) and what you guess.

Language

In Chapter 3, Pip takes the food and file he has stolen to the convict:

> The mist was heavier yet when I got out upon the marshes, so that instead of my running at everything, everything seemed to run at me. [...] The gates and dykes and banks came bursting at me through the mist, as if they cried as plainly as could be, 'A boy with Somebody-else's pork pie! Stop him!'

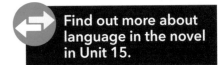

Find out more about language in the novel in Unit 15.

1 Write down eight words from this extract that make the landscape seem frightening and menacing.

In Chapter 5, the convict Pip has helped comes across another escaped convict and fights him:

Water was splashing, and mud was flying, and oaths were being sworn, and blows were being struck, when some more men went down into the ditch to help the sergeant, and dragged out, separately, my convict and the other one. Both were bleeding and panting.

2 a Copy the extract and highlight all the words associated with violence.

b Underline the words ending in '-ing'. What effect do these words have?

Plot and structure

At the end of Chapter 7, Pip has to temporarily leave Joe to visit Miss Havisham at Satis House:

I had never parted from him before, and what with my feelings and what with soap-suds, I could at first see no stars from the chaise-cart. But they twinkled out one by one, without throwing any light on the questions why on earth I was going to play at Miss Havisham's, and what on earth I was expected to play at.

1 As with the entrance of the convict, Miss Havisham's entrance is going to trigger events that affect the rest of the story. What do you think will happen next? Work in groups and discuss whether you think Dickens drops some hints about what these events might be towards the end of Chapter 7.

 Find out more about plot and structure in the novel in Unit 11.

 Learning checkpoint

Look back over your work so far and write:

a a paragraph about Pip's character
b a paragraph about the setting of the novel.

Use supporting detail from the text in your paragraphs.

GETTING IT INTO WRITING

In your exam you will answer a question about *Great Expectations*. The format of these questions will be consistent. The first part of the question will make clear the part of the text provided, and the subject to be focused on. Then there will be two bullets, making clear that the answer should be based on the extract, and on the novel as a whole. The format of the question is like this:

In an extract from (Chapter X) Dickens describes (person, situation, event, place, relationship, emotions, etc.). Write about:

- **how he presents the (person, situation, event, place, relationship, emotions, etc.) in that extract**
- **how the (person, situation, event, place, relationship, emotions) are presented in the novel as a whole.**

The text lasso

Throughout the book, you will practise answering questions like this. To do so, you will need to choose extracts that are about 300 words long to write about. To find an extract of this length, follow these steps:

- Open your copy of the novel to any page and count a 300-word section.
- Lay a piece of paper over your page and mark out the space of the 300-word section.
- Take the paper off the page and cut around your markings. You now have a hole in the paper that is about the size of 300 words.
- Lay this piece of paper over any page in the novel to select a 300-word extract of your choice.

Writing about Pip as a character

Look through Chapters 1 and 2. Choose an incident that reveals something about Pip's character: perhaps the convict's seizing him or his theft of the pie. Find a quotation at the centre of your chosen incident that seems worth noting. Now lay your text lasso over the page so that the key quotation is roughly in the middle. Move it about a little so that the extract coincides with the beginnings and endings of sentences.

Now complete these activities using the extract you have chosen.

1 Summarise your extract in one sentence.

2 Explain in a single sentence why your chosen extract is a key event in the chapter.

GETTING FURTHER

Considering the convict

Here, at the start of the novel, we do not know the convict's personal story or what his home looks like. He is just a strange, violent character who has burst into Pip's story. Later, we discover that his name is Magwitch. What are we to make of him at this point in the novel?

1 Do you think Magwitch is:

a   cruel by nature
b   made cruel and violent by things that have happened to him
c   driven to cruelty by circumstances and need?

2 What do you think will be the impact of this event on Pip's life and his character?

3 When Pip steals the file and the 'wittles', he commits the kind of crime for which people were sent to prison or even executed at the time the novel was written. Write a paragraph explaining how Dickens uses this event to comment on the conditions of the poor in 19th-century society.

Thinking ahead

In this unit, you have looked at how setting and character are connected at the beginning of *Great Expectations*. As you read on, keep looking for this connection – for example note the dark, sinister setting of Satis House in Chapter 8. Throughout the book, you will find that the settings reveal something about the characters that inhabit them.

Learning checkpoint

Write a paragraph that explains how your chosen extract helps you to understand Pip's character. Use one quotation from the text as evidence.

How will I know I've done this well?

✔ Comment on specific words or phrases used in the text.

✔ Explain something about Pip's character.

✔ Include some details about his relationship with other characters, for example his sister, Joe or the convict.

✔ Use accurate spelling and clear, well-punctuated sentences.

2

Satis House: Pip meets Miss Havisham and Estella

How does Dickens use language to establish and develop character?

Your progress in this unit:

- analyse how Dickens establishes Miss Havisham's character
- investigate the language he uses to do this
- put different characters in the hot-seat to interpret their perspective
- write a detailed essay plan for a question about the novel.

GETTING STARTED – THE STORY AND YOU

Pip is taken to see Miss Havisham – a wealthy, eccentric old lady who lives in a derelict mansion called Satis House. He is led into a dark drawing room by Estella, a beautiful but cruel and cold girl. Meeting these two **characters** marks a turning point in Pip's life.

Recounting past events

Great Expectations begins with an older man writing about himself as a young boy. In this way, Pip has two roles in the **novel – narrator** and character.

1 Do you remember visiting someone such as a distant relation or going somewhere for the first time?

   a   Write a paragraph about that visit.
   b   When you have finished, re-read your work. Underline any words or phrases that indicate that these are the memories of an older person looking back.

GETTING CLOSER – FOCUS ON DETAILS

How does Dickens start to develop the narrative?

Read through the key details and quotations from Chapters 8–17 to get an overview of the section you are about to explore.

   Watch characters from the novel summarise Chapters 8–17 on Cambridge Elevate.

1 The one-line summaries for Chapters 9, 10 and 11 are missing from the chart. Skim-read the chapters and write your own one-line summary for each.

Chapter 8
Pip is taken to Satis House to visit Miss Havisham.

The cold wind seemed to blow colder there, than outside the gate.

Chapter 9
'Pretty well?' Mr. Pumblechook repeated. 'Pretty well is no answer. Tell us what you mean by pretty well, boy?'

Chapter 11
'Come here! You may kiss me, if you like.'

Chapter 10
When the fights were over, Biddy gave out the number of a page, and then we all read aloud what we could – or what we couldn't.

Chapter 12
Pip continues to visit Satis House.

Miss Havisham would often ask me in a whisper, or when we were alone, 'Does she grow prettier and prettier, Pip?'

Chapter 13
Miss Havisham pays for Pip to be apprenticed to Joe.

It was quite in vain for me to endeavour to make him sensible that he ought to speak to Miss Havisham.

Chapter 14
Pip hates his apprenticeship.

It is a most miserable thing to feel ashamed of home.

Chapter 15
Mrs Joe is attacked, and Pip finds her lying unconscious.

I became aware of my sister – lying without sense or movement on the bare boards where she had been knocked down by a tremendous blow on the back of the head, dealt by some unknown hand.

Chapter 16
Biddy is paid to take care of Mrs Joe.

'Why, of course!' cried Biddy, with an exultant face. 'Don't you see? It's *him*!'

Chapter 17
Pip tells Biddy he loves Estella and he wants to be a gentleman.

'It may be all quite true,' said I to Biddy, 'but I admire her dreadfully.'

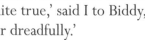

First impressions of Miss Havisham

Characterisation is the process by which writers establish and develop characters. Typically, a novelist tells the reader up to five different things about a character:

- what they and their home look like
- what they say
- what they do
- what they think
- how others respond to them, both in their presence and when they are not there.

1 Re-read Chapter 8, paying close attention to Miss Havisham. When you have finished, list:

a six words **that she speaks** that sum up her character at this point in the novel
b eight words **that Dickens uses** to describe her that best characterise her.

2 Now write two or three sentences describing your first impressions of Miss Havisham's character.

Investigating character – Pip and Miss Havisham

1 Get into groups of four in preparation for a 'silent discussion'. Choose to investigate **either** Pip **or** Miss Havisham.

a Place a large sheet of paper in the centre of the table and write the name of your chosen character in the middle of it.
b In silence, note down any ideas you have about the character based on your reading of the novel up to Chapter 17. Include a quotation or page number from the chapter to support each idea.

c Afterwards, read the notes that other members of your group have made and comment on them – but **only in writing**. If you agree with someone, want to challenge them, want to ask someone to explain what they mean – write down your question. This way, the whole discussion is on paper. The notes you have made will help you with the writing task at the end of the unit.

2 Stay in the same groups. You are going to put Pip and Miss Havisham in the hot-seat to find out more about them.

a Individually, write down six questions that you would like to ask Miss Havisham and six questions that you would like to ask Pip.
b Arrange one chair with three others facing it. Take it in turns to sit in the hot-seat in role as one of the characters and answer the questions put to you by the rest of the group.
c As a questioner, make notes of the answers that the character gives.

Watch Estella in the hot-seat on Cambridge Elevate.

Watch Miss Havisham in the hot-seat on Cambridge Elevate.

PUTTING DETAILS TO USE

Character and characterisation

Now that you have an understanding of how Dickens presents the character of Miss Havisham, you need to gather evidence to see whether you can support your interpretation of her. She first appears in Chapter 8, and then again in Chapters 11, 12 and 13. Re-read these chapters.

1 When Pip first visits Satis House, he describes Miss Havisham:

> I saw that the bride within the bridal dress had withered like the dress, and like the flowers, and had no brightness left but the brightness of her sunken eyes.

a What does the bridal dress tell us about Miss Havisham's character?

b How do we know that Miss Havisham is unhappy?

2 When Dickens describes a character's costume and where they live, he is writing about their choices and their fate. You can interpret these descriptions as though Dickens were partly writing about the characters themselves.

a Which descriptions in Chapter 8 show that Miss Havisham is rich?

b Write down three quotations that make Miss Havisham seem ghost-like.

c How does Dickens make Miss Havisham seem sinister? Explain this in three sentences. Think about her appearance, including her clothes, where she lives, and what she says and does.

Key terms

characterisation: the way in which writers establish and develop characters by describing features that are unique or distinctive.

interpretation: your understanding of the meaning of what characters say and do.

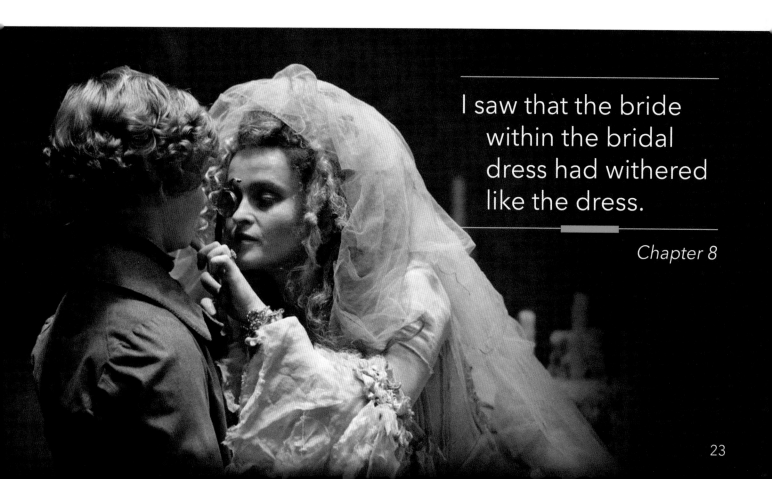

I saw that the bride within the bridal dress had withered like the dress.

Chapter 8

Language and characterisation

1 Look at this short **dialogue** between Pip and Miss Havisham:

'Do you know what I touch here?' [...]
'Yes, ma'am.' [...]
'What do I touch?'
'Your heart.'
'Broken!'
She uttered the word with an eager look, and with strong emphasis, and with a weird smile that had a kind of boast in it.

a What does the exclamation '**Broken!**' suggest about Miss Havisham?

b Choose five words to describe the language she uses when she speaks to Pip (e.g. rude, polite, sharp, charming, cunning, confused or something else).

c When Miss Havisham points to her heart, Pip remembers the second convict he encountered in the graveyard. What makes him remember that episode? How would you interpret that sudden memory?

Key terms

dialogue: a conversation between two or more people in a piece of writing.

Character and motive

1 Pip becomes enthralled with Estella:

'Am I pretty?'
'Yes; I think you are very pretty.'
'Am I insulting?'
'Not so much so as you were last time,' said I.
'Not so much so?'
'No.'
She fired when she asked the last question, and she slapped my face with such force as she had, when I answered it.
'Now?' said she. 'You little coarse monster, what do you think of me now?'

What does this episode tell us about the relationship between Estella and Pip?

2 Chapter 11 marks Estella's second appearance in the book. What do we know about her so far?

a Make notes on passages in Chapters 8-17 where she is present or where others talk about her. (Remember the five ways in which a novelist can tell us about a character that you looked at earlier in this unit.)

b What does the information you have gathered reveal about Estella herself and about Dickens's methods and intentions?

Miss Havisham's personality and social standing have a strong effect on first Pip and then Joe.

In Chapter 9, Pip returns from his first visit to Satis House and is questioned by Uncle Pumblechook and Mrs Joe. At first, the boy cannot think what to say, but then he describes his visit as a series of wild fancies.

3 Why do you think that Pip does not give an accurate account of events? Think about:

a the differences between his own home and family and those of the people he has just visited

b his experience of Estella (he refers to this himself when explaining to Joe later that his story '**ain't true**')

c Pip's own confused explanation of how he came to tell such lies.

In Chapter 13, Pip and Joe return from a visit to Satis House and are again questioned by Uncle Pumblechook and Mrs Joe.

4 This time it is Joe who gives an inaccurate account of what Miss Havisham said.

a In what ways does Joe change the conversation he had with Miss Havisham when he reports it to his wife and uncle?

b Why do you think Joe does not report his conversation accurately?

⇄ Find out more about character and characterisation in the novel in Unit 13.

 Learning checkpoint

Choose a 300-word extract that will allow you to further investigate Miss Havisham's character. Write down the chapter number, the page number, and the opening and closing sentences of your extract. Using your extract, carry out these activities:

a Explain what your extract reveals about Miss Havisham in general terms.

b Write down two quotations that reveal something about Miss Havisham's character.

c Explain the quotations.

d Choose four words from your extract that sum up Miss Havisham's attitudes.

e Explain why you think Dickens has used these words.

f Write two or three paragraphs about the relationship between Pip and Miss Havisham.

How will I know I've done this well?

✔ Comment on specific words or phrases used in the text.

✔ Explain something about Miss Havisham's character.

✔ Include some details about the relationship between Pip and Miss Havisham.

✔ Interrogate the language used in detail.

✔ Use accurate spelling and clear, well-punctuated sentences.

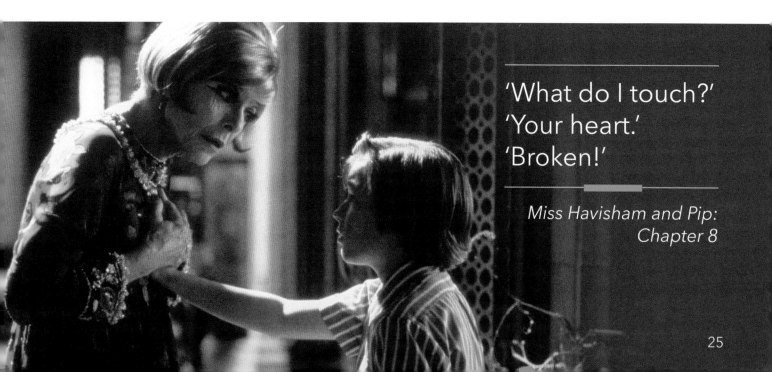

'What do I touch?'
'Your heart.'
'Broken!'

Miss Havisham and Pip: Chapter 8

GETTING IT INTO WRITING

Writing about Pip and Miss Havisham as characters

Throughout this unit, you have gathered notes about the characters of Pip and Miss Havisham. Now you will use these to produce a detailed essay plan for this question:

Starting with this extract, write about how Dickens introduces the character of Miss Havisham. Write about:

- **how Dickens presents Miss Havisham in this extract**
- **how Dickens presents the character of Miss Havisham in the first part of the novel.**

Plan your essay

1 Use your text lasso to choose an extract. You can use the same one you selected for the Learning checkpoint activity in this unit, or a different one. Then use your time as follows:

- **4 minutes:** make a spider diagram of all that you have found out about Miss Havisham.
- **1 minute:** gather three quotations from the extract.
- **30 seconds:** underline ideas that seem particularly strong.
- **30 seconds:** cross out ideas that seem irrelevant.
- **1 minute:** number the ideas to plan which you are going to write about first, second, third, and so on.

Use the notes you have made throughout this unit to help you.

 Complete this assignment on Cambridge Elevate.

Learning checkpoint

Compare your plan with that of another student. Discuss the similarities and differences, and select three ideas:

a of yours that you can recommend to your partner

b of theirs that you can copy or learn from.

How will I know I've done this well?

✔ **The best answers** will offer well-written interpretations of the evidence in specific scenes, commenting on what Miss Havisham says and does, how other people react to her, and what this reveals about her personality. They may discuss how a 19th-century reader might respond to an episode or show the relevance of information about what was happening in England at the time.

✔ **Good answers** will show a clear understanding of how Dickens characterises Miss Havisham, using well-chosen examples from a number of episodes in the novel. They may comment on specific words or phrases used in the text. They will use accurate spelling and clear, well-punctuated sentences.

✔ **Weaker answers** will comment on Miss Havisham in general, using few or no specific examples and without mentioning why Dickens might use them or how they might affect the readership.

GETTING FURTHER

Write your essay

1 If you feel confident with your plan, you could challenge yourself further by trying to write your essay. (You will find more guidance on essay writing in later units.)

a Arrange your plan and notes from the unit in front of you, and start writing.

b Check your work when you have finished.

c Compare your finished essay with a partner and learn from anything you think they are doing better than you.

 Contexts

Is *Great Expectations* autobiographical? Critics agree that Dickens had put into Pip memories of himself as a child. He is even believed to have started writing an autobiography at the time, then stopped and written this novel instead.

However, Pip was born into a working-class family, where Joe Gargery works with his hands and tools. Dickens's father was a shipping clerk and worked in an office, which put him at the bottom of the Victorian middle classes. When his father was imprisoned for debt, the 12-year-old Dickens had to leave school and get a job. He worked 10-hour days packing pots of boot polish and putting on labels. This made him very conscious of the line between being rich and being poor, and how people might climb from one social class to another – or fall down.

Dickens was very concerned about the treatment of children and many of his novels deal with the issue of neglect and child labour. How might he have reacted to these issues in the world today?

3

Pip's fortune

How does Mr Jaggers's visit change the course of Pip's life?

GETTING STARTED – THE STORY AND YOU

Mr Jaggers, a lawyer, comes to the village bearing life-changing news for Pip: he has been given a large fortune. He must give up his life with Joe and go to London, where he will learn to be a gentleman. There is a condition attached – Pip must never try to find out the identity of his secret benefactor.

Coming into money

1 A representative from a reality TV show visits your house. They would like you to be the focus of a ten-year television series, which will broadcast one episode a year.

You will be given an education at Dickens College, one of the most expensive boarding schools in the country. You will have to live at the school as a boarder. Your education, your food and clothing will be paid for. You will receive an allowance of £400 per month.

But there are conditions: you must never tell anyone that the TV show has paid for your education, and every year you must take part in a half-hour television documentary. Would you go?

a Discuss this opportunity in small groups.
b Draw a table showing what you would gain and what you would lose.

GETTING CLOSER – FOCUS ON DETAILS

Read through the key details and quotations from Chapters 18–24 to get an overview of the section you are about to explore.

 Watch characters from the novel summarise chapters 18–24 on Cambridge Elevate.

1 The quotations for chapters 18, 19 and 20 are missing from the chart. Skim-read these chapters and choose a quotation that you think sums them up. Discuss your quotations with others and decide which fits best.

Chapter 18
The lawyer Mr Jaggers comes to the village and informs Pip that he is to be educated as a gentleman and will inherit a large sum of money.

Chapter 19
Pip prepares for his new life and then departs for London.

Chapter 20
Mr Jaggers informs Pip about his living arrangements at Barnard's Inn.

Chapter 22
Herbert Pocket turns out to be the pale young gentleman whom Pip had once fought at Satis House, and he tells Pip Miss Havisham's story.

'The day came, but not the bridegroom.'

Chapter 21
Pip meets his new roommate, Herbert Pocket.

'I am sure I shall be very happy to show London to you.'

Chapter 23
Pip meets Mr Pocket, Herbert's father, who is to be his tutor.

Mr. Pocket had been educated at Harrow and at Cambridge, where he had distinguished himself.

Chapter 24
Wemmick invites Pip over for dinner and refers to Jaggers's housekeeper as a **'tamed beast'**.

'Take Mr. Pip's written order, and pay him twenty pounds.'

The big story

As a young man, Dickens worked as a journalist. Imagine that, like Dickens, you are a young and enthusiastic journalist for *The Globe* newspaper. The editor calls you into his office and tells you to go down to the marshes to report the story of the blacksmith's apprentice who is about to become a gentleman.

1 Prepare to interview the main **characters** by writing two or three questions each for Pip, Joe and Pumblechook. Look closely at Chapter 18 and use phrases from the book to help you frame your questions.

2 Work with another student. Take it in turns to role-play the journalist and the characters.

   a As the journalist, make quick notes of the answers you are given. Always keep in mind the front-page story you want to write.

   b As the characters, think about the following:

- **Pip:** will you be excited, or innocent, or too shy to talk to the press?
- **Joe:** what will be your attitude towards the press and to events? Will you be happy at Pip's news or sad to be losing a friend?
- **Uncle Pumblechook:** will you be only too delighted to promote your own importance? Will you understand the events properly or make mistakes?

3 Work with another student. Role-play the meeting that takes place between the journalist and the editor when the journalist returns from the interview. Refer to the notes you have made: what is the most important thing you have found out?

 Meet the editor of *The Globe* and find out your assignment on Cambridge Elevate.

4 Now write your front-page story. Your editor wants a headline and 250 words of text. Write the story in formal, modern English.

5 For a greater challenge, look closely at Dickens's language in the **novel**, then rewrite your news article in the style of the author.

PUTTING DETAILS TO USE

Chapters 18–24 of *Great Expectations* are about Pip leaving his home on the marshes and starting a new life in London.

Mr Jaggers's language

1 Mr Jaggers's visit in Chapter 18 is one of the most important events in the novel. Jaggers tells Pip that he is about to become a gentleman. Look closely at the language he uses:

> 'Further, that it is the desire of the present possessor of that property, that he be immediately removed from his present sphere of life and from this place, and be brought up as a gentleman – in a word, as a young fellow of great expectations.'

   a Write down three words which Jaggers uses that are formal and complex – the type that a lawyer might use (e.g. '**possessor**').

   b Find three quotations that seem to be typical of the language Jaggers uses (e.g. '**I am instructed to communicate to him**').

   c Write a paragraph explaining why you think Jaggers uses this language when he is telling Pip such exciting news. Give examples of the way that this language makes him seem distant and unemotional.

 Find out more about language in the novel in Unit 15.

Character and characterisation

Think about the significance of this news to Pip and Joe.

1 Write Joe's thoughts in two or three sentences as he hears the news. You could begin with this phrase:

'I'm excited and confusedly all a-stammer because …'

2 **'Miss Havisham was going to make my fortune on a grand scale.'** Give three reasons why Pip thinks that the secret benefactor is Miss Havisham (e.g. she is the only wealthy person he knows).

3 When he has told Pip the news, Mr Jaggers begins referring to him as 'Mr Pip'. Write two bullet points summarising the significance of this.

 Find out more about character and characterisation in the novel in Unit 13.

Characters and ideas

1 In Chapter 19, Pip sets out for London. Towards the end of the chapter, he says that he did not want Joe to walk with him to the coach road:

I am afraid – sore afraid – that this purpose originated in my sense of the contrast there would be between me and Joe.

a What do you think is implied in this extract?
b What does it suggest about Pip's changing attitudes?
c Why is he '**sore afraid**'?

2 At the beginning of Chapter 20, Pip arrives at Jaggers's office. Re-read this section, noting how Dickens describes this **setting**.

What do you think of the description Dickens gives? Write some notes. You could use some of the following words to help you:

detailed	criminal	sarcastic
surprise	interesting	friendly
creepy	rich	humorous
law	dirty	cynical
poor	formal	informal

'a young fellow of great expectations.'

Mr Jaggers: Chapter 18

Themes and ideas

Through Pip's journey, Dickens shows different aspects of being a gentleman. By the end of the novel, we reach the conclusion that it is, in fact, not about birth, education, job or wealth. Being a gentleman is not a social or economic quality at all – it is a moral and religious one.

Contexts

The Industrial Revolution created new ways to make money. By Dickens's time, some people had taken advantage of the new manufacturing industries so much that they were as wealthy as the aristocracy. This new wealthy class wanted to be considered 'gentlemen' – a term that emphasised several qualities:

- **Birth:** the aristocracy were gentlemen because of their family connections.
- **School:** men who had gone to public schools were gentlemen because of their education.
- **Job:** clergymen, military officers and MPs were gentlemen because of their occupation.
- **Wealth:** gentleman tended to inherit land and money.

Men who had made their own fortune, rather than inheriting it, were not always accepted as 'gentlemen'. Born into a middle-class family and then sent to a working-class job, Dickens grew up wanting to regain that lost status. However, he also questioned its value.

 1 Choose a 300-word extract from Chapters 18–24. Write four questions about it, dealing with:

- a   plot
- b   character
- c   setting
- d   language.

✔ Learning checkpoint

Swap your extract and your questions with a partner. Answer the questions about their chosen extract. Once you have both finished, mark each other's work, using the following checklist:

- ✔ Comment on specific words or phrases used in the text.
- ✔ Explain something about plot, character, setting and language.
- ✔ Include specific details.
- ✔ Write in a formal, critical style.
- ✔ Use accurate spelling and clear, well-punctuated sentences.

GETTING IT INTO WRITING

Working with quotations

When you write about a piece of literature, you are expected to use quotations. Quotations are the evidence that proves your opinions are based on a study of the book. A good quotation should be short and to the point.

… this purpose originated in my sense of the contrast there would be between me and Joe.

Chapter 19

Look at this question:

Starting with this extract, explain why the news that Mr Jaggers brings is so significant for Pip. Write about:

- **how Dickens presents the news in this extract**
- **how Dickens shows how the news is significant in the novel as a whole.**

You might want to use this quotation as evidence:

My dream was out; my wild fancy was surpassed by sober reality; Miss Havisham was going to make my fortune on a grand scale.

Once you have used your quotation, you should add some commentary in which you interpret your evidence. For example:

Pip's life is about to change. The money and the fortune that he had dreamed of as a small boy are to be his. The simple language of the opening statement, 'My dream was out,' is balanced by the more complex language of the older author looking back, 'surpassed by sober reality'.

 Complete this assignment on Cambridge Elevate.

1 Copy out three further quotations that you could use as evidence in the writing task. Write two or three sentences to interpret each of your quotations.

GETTING FURTHER

What is a gentleman?

1 Here is a Victorian attempt to define a gentleman in terms of what he can do:

It is the duty of a gentleman to know how to ride, to shoot, to fence, to box, to swim, to row and to dance. He should be graceful. If attacked by ruffians, a man should be able to defend himself, and also to defend women from their insults.

Rules of Etiquette and Home Culture, 1886

What connections do you see with **themes**, characters and events in *Great Expectations*?

 Watch an interview with a Victorian gentleman on Cambridge Elevate.

2 In Chapter 19, Pip visits several shops to order clothes. He announces his change of fortunes to Mr Trabb the tailor. Notice:

a Mr Trabbs's change of attitude and language

b the use of the expressions '**nobility and gentry**' and '**London gentleman**'

c the response of his unnamed assistant, Trabb's boy.

Write a short paragraph about the theme of social class in this scene.

 Key terms

theme: an idea that a writer keeps returning to, exploring it form different perspectives.

4

Pip's new life in London

How does Pip's personality develop in London?

Your progress in this unit:
- look closely at Pip's life in London, and at his new and old friends
- examine Dickens's use of language in this extract
- produce a pitch for a computer game – Wemmick's Castle
- write an essay.

GETTING STARTED - THE STORY AND YOU

Wemmick, Mr Jaggers's bill collector, invites Pip to visit him at his house in Walworth. While at work in the City with Mr Jaggers, Wemmick is sombre and unfriendly. However, when Pip visits him at his home, he finds him to be completely the opposite.

Does where we live reflect who we are?

1 People's personalities are often reflected in their home. Describe the place where you live to a classmate. How does it reflect your personality?

2 People can behave differently in different situations and different company. Do you behave differently at college or school from how you are at home? If so, how? Discuss this with a partner.

3 Think about the most eccentric or unusual person that you have ever met. Imagine you go to visit them in their home. Write a short description of this visit (one or two paragraphs). You could include:

a arriving and entering the house
b details about the house and the objects in it, in particular anything unusual
c something your host said
d meeting anyone else in the house (another family member, for example).

When you have finished, compare your description with those of other students.

4 Now re-read Chapter 25, focusing on Pip's impressions of Wemmick and his visit to his home.

GETTING CLOSER - FOCUS ON DETAILS

Read through the following summary of Chapters 25–38 to get an overview of the section you are about to explore.

 Watch characters from the novel summarise chapters 25–38 on Cambridge Elevate.

1 Look at the chart summarising the content of each chapter in this section. Scan each chapter and find a key quotation for each one.

Chapter 25
Wemmick shows himself to be completely different at home than he is at work.

Chapter 26
Pip meets Bentley Drummle at a dinner held by Jaggers.

Chapter 29
Miss Havisham encourages Pip to love Estella.

Chapter 28
Pip resolves to go to home, but he stays at the Blue Boar without even seeing Joe.

Chapter 27
Joe comes to London to visit Pip.

Chapter 30
Pip confesses to Herbert his love for Estella and his guilt at not visiting Joe.

Chapter 31
Pip and Herbert go to watch Mr Wopsle perform in *Hamlet*.

Chapter 32
Wemmick takes Pip on a tour of Newgate prison.

Chapter 33
Estella leads Pip to believe that there is an 'arrangement' for the two of them.

Chapter 34
Pip receives news that Mrs Joe has died.

Chapter 35
Pip returns home for his sister's funeral and vows to visit more often.

Chapter 36
Pip turns 21 and begins receiving an annual income of 500 pounds.

Chapter 38
Estella tells Pip that Bentley Drummle is courting her.

Chapter 37
Pip decides to help Herbert establish his business.

Wemmick's Castle

Shakespeare learnt about plays in school and he went on to write some of the best plays the world has ever seen. Dickens hit on the idea of serialising his **novels** in magazines. Great writers discover new and exciting ways for audiences to access literature. Some people believe that video games are the new vehicle for narrative.

1 'Wemmick's Castle' will be a video game based on Pip's visit to Wemmick's house in Chapter 25 of *Great Expectations*. You have been invited to write a proposal for the game design. This should include:

    a A **storyboard** of the game, including:
- drawings of at least four frames
- at least eight elements from Dickens's text
- a paragraph or two to describe what is going on.

    b A proposal for how the game is played (200–400 words), making clear and specific reference to the text of the novel.

The target audience is young people between the ages of 15 and 18. The design should be credible but, most importantly, the game must help students to find out about this episode in *Great Expectations*.

PUTTING DETAILS TO USE

The following activities will help you focus on some of the detail of the text in this middle section of the novel. Note down your answers to use later in the unit and for revision.

Character and characterisation

In Chapter 25, Pip visits Wemmick's home. This is a humorous and unusual **interlude** – a departure from the main plot of the novel.

1 The house itself tells us a lot about its owner.

    a What does Wemmick's drawbridge reveal about his attitude towards a man's home?

    b Wemmick thinks that '**if you have any idea carry it out and keep it up**'. Find three descriptions of his home that illustrate this idea.

2 When Dickens brings together Pip and Wemmick, he is encouraging us to **contrast** the two young men. Write four bullet points showing the ways in which Wemmick's situation is different from Pip's. You could start with the following:

Wemmick has to work hard at the office, whereas Pip doesn't have to work at all.

Language

Look at this extract:

Then, he conducted me to a bower about a dozen yards off, but which was approached by such ingenious twists of path that it took quite a long time to get at.

Here, Dickens uses a **mock-heroic** style, which makes small things seem grand and – in this case – makes Wemmick appear comical. It is a technique Dickens often uses.

1 Write down three more examples from Chapter 25 where Dickens uses the mock-heroic style (e.g. '**out of sight so as not to impede the idea of fortification**').

2 What do you think Pip's attitude is to Wemmick and his home life? How do you know this? Support your ideas with evidence from the text. You might want to use some of these words in your answer:

amused	love	family
confused	home	comfort

3 Now try writing in the mock-heroic style yourself. Describe a goal in a recent game of playground football as though it had happened in the Premier League. Mention the players' transfer values and the reaction of the crowd.

🔑 Key terms

storyboard: a sequence of drawings that show the different scenes in a story or levels in a video game.

interlude: a scene or event that provides a break from the main action of a story.

contrast: to point out the ways in which two or more things are different from each other.

mock-heroic: writing in which the style is too formal or dramatic for the subject-matter.

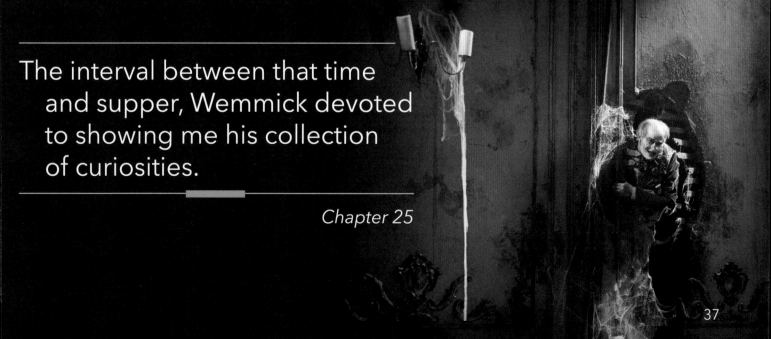

The interval between that time and supper, Wemmick devoted to showing me his collection of curiosities.

Chapter 25

Characters and themes

In Chapter 27, Joe visits Pip in London. Pip worries about how he will find the contrast between his old life and his new one:

As the time approached I should have liked to run away.

The day of Joe's visit arrives:

I heard Joe on the staircase. I knew it was Joe, by his clumsy manner of coming up-stairs – his state boots being always too big for him – and by the time it took him to read the names on the other floors in the course of his ascent.

 Pip seems to be embarrassed by his old friend. Write three bullet points explaining how we know this. Look closely at how Dickens's use of language tells us this. For example:

Pip says he wanted to run away. This suggests he is anxious because …

Joined by Pip's friend, Herbert, they eat a meal together and Pip notices the way Joe eats:

[He] dropped so much more than he ate, and pretended that he hadn't dropped it; that I was heartily glad when Herbert left us for the city.

2 Write a short paragraph explaining why you think Pip is glad that Herbert has to leave. Remember to present the evidence and interpret it.

Language

Joe tells Pip that Miss Havisham wishes to see him. Look closely at the use of language in the following extract:

'Which I say, Sir,' replied Joe, with an air of legal formality, as if he were making his will, 'Miss A., or otherways Havisham. Her expression air then as follering: "Mr Gargery. You air in correspondence with Mr Pip?" Having had a letter from you I were able to say "I am." '

1 a List the expressions that Joe repeats in this scene. What do they mean? Does he use them in earlier scenes?
   b Why does Dickens spell many of Joe's words incorrectly?
   c Analyse why Joe speaks with '**an air of legal formality**'.

Character and characterisation

In Chapter 38, Estella continues to be cold and distant, but she is clearly trying to tell Pip something:

'Pip, Pip,' she said one evening, coming to such a check, when we sat apart at a darkening window of the house in Richmond; 'will you never take warning?'
'Of what?'
'Of me.'
'Warning not to be attracted by you, do you mean, Estella?'
'Do I mean! If you don't know what I mean, you are blind.'

 Find out more about character and characterisation in the novel in Unit 13.

1. We are slowly learning more about Estella, but she remains in many ways a mystery at this point in the novel. Make notes addressing the following questions.

   a   Does Estella really want to push Pip away? If so, why?
   b   Is Estella truly as cold as she appears to be? If so, why?
   c   Is Estella trying to protect Pip? If so, from what?

2. Despite her cruelty, Pip continues to pursue Estella's love. Do you think he is doing the right thing? Write two or three sentences explaining your opinion. Back up your ideas with evidence from the text.

Estella and Pip visit Miss Havisham, where Pip sees the two women disagree for the first time:

'So hard, so hard!' moaned Miss Havisham, with her former action.
'Who taught me to be hard?' returned Estella. 'Who praised me when I learnt my lesson?'

3. Write three or four bullet points explaining what you think Estella is suggesting about her upbringing. For example:

Miss Havisham never showed Estella any love.

'Who taught me to be hard?'

Estella: Chapter 38

GETTING IT INTO WRITING

How does Dickens present Wemmick?

All Dickens's **characters** – even those that only play a small part in the story – are sharply drawn, with lively, interesting details. In this activity, you are going to write about Wemmick and, in particular, the way in which his character is reflected in his surroundings.

Look at this question:

Examine how Dickens presents Wemmick's character. Write about:

- **the link between character and setting**
- **the language Dickens uses to portray this.**

1 Look at the following beginning of an essay plan. The points are in the wrong order.

> Link between characters and setting.
>
> Language, e.g. 'It was protected by an ingenious little tarpaulin contrivance in the nature of an umbrella.'
>
> Wemmick's attention to detail; clever at making do with what is available.
>
> Wemmick's character in Newgate.
>
> Pip finds Wemmick a different character at home.
>
> Wemmick befriends criminals; 'portable property'.
>
> Three or four details of Wemmick's house: explain what these tell us about Wemmick's character.
>
> Wemmick harsh, business-like and uncaring.

Put this list in order to create the beginning of a usable essay plan. Finish the plan with your own ideas, then write an essay in answer to the question. When you have finished, spend five minutes checking back over your writing.

 Complete this assignment on Cambridge Elevate.

Learning checkpoint

Now that you have worked with a range of details from the text, you need next to show how well you can understand and interpret those details in your written work.

Use your text lasso to select an event from Chapters 25–38 (you may want to use an episode that you have studied in this unit). Write down the chapter number, the page number, and the opening and closing sentences of your extract.

Using your extract, answer these questions about Pip's new life in London:

a Explain what your extract is about in general terms.

b Write down two or three quotations that reveal something about the characters and setting.

c Explain these quotations.

d Write two or three sentences explaining the importance of this event to the plot of the novel as a whole.

How will I know I've done this well?

✔ **The best answers** will show knowledge by putting the episode in the **context** of the developing plot. They will show good analytical skills by exploring how Dickens uses language. They will show good interpretative skills by commenting on characterisation and setting. They will offer personal opinions based on evidence from the text.

✔ **Good answers** will demonstrate knowledge and clear understanding of what Dickens does in the episode. They will use well-chosen examples from the extract and refer to other events in the novel. They will offer personal opinions.

✔ **Weaker answers** will only comment on the events in the extract. They may mention other episodes, but will tend to recount the plot rather than interpret the evidence. They will comment on characters as real people, rather than as Dickens's constructs.

GETTING FURTHER

Identity is a recurring **theme** in *Great Expectations*. As you study the novel, make a note of where the theme occurs. Unit 14 will help with this further.

While Pip has rejected his home and is searching for a better life, Wemmick is very secure in himself. He has developed a technique for coping with life: he is a different character at home and at work. Dickens uses this narrative technique of mirroring throughout the novel:

- Estella and Pip are both orphans being brought up in emotionally challenging circumstances.
- Magwitch and Compeyson are both convicts.
- Herbert and Joe are both Pip's friends.

1 List other examples of mirroring in the novel.

2 Write a paragraph explaining what you think Dickens is trying to achieve with this technique.

 Key terms

context: the historical circumstances of a piece of writing, which affect what an author wrote and the way they wrote it.

5 The benefactor discovered

How does Dickens weave themes into his narrative?

Your progress in this unit:
- interpret the themes of crime and justice, and ambition and self-improvement
- take part in a debate about Magwitch's actions in the novel
- write a detailed essay plan for a practice question.

GETTING STARTED – THE STORY AND YOU

One stormy night, Pip is sitting alone when he hears footsteps. He takes a candle and goes to the top of the stairs. From the darkness, a stranger emerges. He is '**roughly**' dressed and has long grey hair – he looks '**like a voyager by sea**'. Pip is horrified to realise that he knows this man.

The unknown benefactor

1 Imagine you meet someone you have not seen for a very long time. How do you think you would recognise them? Their eyes? Their voice? Something else?

After Magwitch has made himself known to Pip, he reveals that he is the source of Pip's wealth. Up to this point, Pip had assumed that the money was from Miss Havisham.

2 Imagine you had received a lot of money or a very valuable gift. You thought you knew who it was from, but then you discover that it is from someone else. The person you thought had given you the gift never gave you any sign that it was not from them. In pairs, discuss the following questions.

  a How would you feel about the person you previously thought had given you the gift?
  b How would you feel about the person who actually did give you the gift?

GETTING CLOSER – FOCUS ON DETAILS

Read through the summaries of Chapters 39–43 to get an overview of the section you are about to explore.

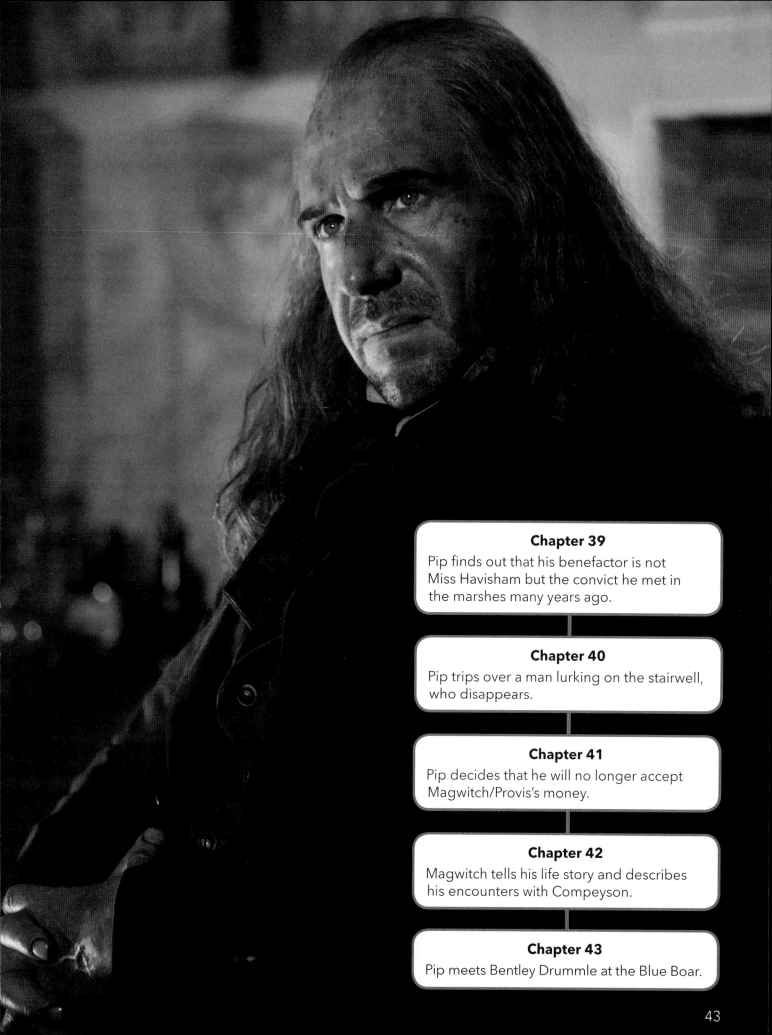

Chapter 39
Pip finds out that his benefactor is not Miss Havisham but the convict he met in the marshes many years ago.

Chapter 40
Pip trips over a man lurking on the stairwell, who disappears.

Chapter 41
Pip decides that he will no longer accept Magwitch/Provis's money.

Chapter 42
Magwitch tells his life story and describes his encounters with Compeyson.

Chapter 43
Pip meets Bentley Drummle at the Blue Boar.

1 Look at the following quotations. Choose which one goes with which chapter in the chart (39–43).

a 'Yet I am afraid the dreadful truth is, Herbert, that he is attached to me, strongly attached to me. Was there ever such a fate!'

b 'Some lawyer, maybe. As to the first letter of that lawyer's name now. Would it be J?'

c Mr Jaggers was at his desk, but, seeing me enter, got up immediately and stood before his fire.
'Now, Pip,' said he, 'be careful.'

d 'No,' said he, 'not particularly. I am going out for a ride in the saddle. I mean to explore those marshes for amusement. Out-of-the-way villages there, they tell me. Curious little public-houses – and smithies – and that. Waiter!'

e 'Young Havisham's name was Arthur. Compeyson is the man who professed to be Miss Havisham's lover.'

Watch characters from the novel summarise Chapters 39–43 on Cambridge Elevate.

A dialectic about Magwitch

A **dialectic** is a formal discussion between two people who take opposite views. In the dialectic, the two participants take it in turns to put forward their ideas and arguments. It is very important that those taking part listen to each other's arguments before responding.

You are going to prepare a dialectic about this statement:

By helping Pip become a gentleman, Magwitch was kind and virtuous.

Watch a sample dialectic about Estella's character on Cambridge Elevate.

1 Work with another student who will be arguing the same view as you. Together, prepare your argument. Then split up to pair with someone who will be offering the opposing argument to you.

a Place two chairs opposite each other and set up a countdown clock.

b The dialectic takes place in three rounds of two minutes each.

c At the end of each round, you can retire to a 'corner' for 30 seconds, where others can help you with more ideas for your side of the argument.

Magwitch – the debate

Hold a class debate on Magwitch's actions. The motion is the same:

By helping Pip become a gentleman, Magwitch was kind and virtuous.

1 Decide whether you agree or disagree with the motion. Write a speech of between 300 and 500 words, using persuasive techniques to try and bring your audience (the house) to your point of view.

If you are arguing **for** the motion, consider these arguments:

- Pip has had a rich life.
- He has met Herbert Pocket, who has been a great friend.
- Had he stayed at the forge, he would have been abused by his sister and Pumblechook.
- Before Magwitch's help, Pip was finding it difficult to learn to read and write.
- If Magwitch had not helped, Pip would not have reached his potential.
- Without Magwitch's help, Pip would not have lived in London and experienced the wider world.
- Would anyone prefer the poverty and squalor of the marshes to the fine clothes and material possessions of life in London?

If you are arguing **against** the motion, consider these arguments:

- Magwitch's actions have interfered with Pip's life and led to his unhappiness.
- Is it right to interfere in anyone's life in such a dramatic way?
- Magwitch kept his help secret, which misled Pip into thinking that Miss Havisham was his benefactor and that he was being prepared to marry Estella.
- Magwitch did not think of the effect his money would have on Pip.
- Magwitch was using Pip to fulfil his own dreams.
- If Pip had stayed at home on the marshes he would have been able to find himself.
- Pip has lived his life as a lie.
- Pip is a hollow man with no identity and no self-knowledge, pathetically in love with an idealised image of a young woman who seems to dislike him.
- Magwitch is too controlling.

2 Choose two people from each side to read their speeches, then hold the debate:

a   The chair introduces the motion to the house (the audience).
b   The house takes a first vote either for or against the motion; individuals can abstain (not vote either way).
c   The results of the first vote are recorded.
d   The house listens to the first speech for the motion.
e   The house listens to the first speech against the motion.
f   The house listens to the second speech for the motion.
g   The house listens to the second speech against the motion.
h   The debate is opened to the floor. At this point, any member of the house can put forward their point of view. The chair chooses who speaks.
i   The house listens to the summary for the motion. This is usually made by the person who gave the first speech for the motion, and should summarise the main points of their argument.
j   The house listens to the summary against the motion.
k   The chair calls for the final vote.
l   The votes are counted and compared with those at the beginning of the debate. Have opinions changed?

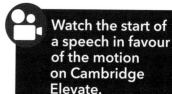

Watch the start of a speech in favour of the motion on Cambridge Elevate.

Key terms

dialectic: an organised discussion between two people who disagree on an issue.

PUTTING DETAILS TO USE

These activities will help you focus on the relationship between Pip and Magwitch. They will also help you think about the **themes** of crime and justice, ambition and self-improvement. Make notes to use later in the unit and for revision.

 Watch a dramatisation of Magwitch's return on Cambridge Elevate.

Characters and perspectives

At the beginning of Chapter 39, on a stormy night, Magwitch pays Pip a visit. In this episode, Pip is frightened by:

- the storm
- the arrival of a stranger who is behaving oddly
- recognising the man who threatened to murder him when he was a child.

1 a How does Dickens create an atmosphere of menace in Chapter 39, even before Magwitch arrives?

b List three ways in which Dickens presents Pip's fear in Chapter 39. For example:

Pip hears someone on the stairs and then a voice from the darkness. He remembers …

2 a Magwitch is not a gentleman. Write down three things he says that show this. For example:

'I wish to come in, Master.' Using the word 'Master' suggests he thinks …

b Write a paragraph about why this is an important moment in Magwitch's life.

3 Read this extract:

I stood, with a hand on the chair-back and a hand on my breast, where I seemed to be suffocating – I stood so, looking wildly at him, until I grasped at the chair, when the room began to surge and turn.

Write three bullet points analysing what causes Pip to feel like this. You may want to mention Miss Havisham and Estella.

Language

In Chapter 40, Magwitch lays a pile of notes on the table and says:

'There's something worth spending in that there book, dear boy. It's yourn. All I've got ain't mine; it's yourn. Don't you be afeerd on it. There's more where that come from. I've come to the old country fur to see my gentleman spend his money *like* a gentleman. That'll be *my* pleasure.'

1 On a copy of the extract, underline four words or phrases that are typical of the language Magwitch uses.

2 Imagine you are Magwitch. Write two paragraphs describing your time in Australia. Make sure you use Magwitch's style of language in your writing.

Character and characterisation

Pip realises as he talks to Herbert in Chapter 41 that, like it or not, there is a strong connection between him and the convict.

Write a short paragraph explaining what you think about Pip and his situation at this point in the novel. Do you feel sorry for him? Do you think he has been foolish or selfish?

Herbert looks at things from Magwitch's point of view:

'… think of this! He comes here at the peril of his life, for the realisation of his fixed idea. In the moment of realisation, after all his toil and waiting, you cut the ground from under his feet, destroy his idea, and make his gains worthless to him. Do you see nothing that he might do, under the disappointment?'

 This is a complex idea expressed in complicated language. Rewrite Herbert's words in plain English. For example:

Look at things from his point of view. He …

Context and setting

In Chapter 42, Magwitch tells his life story, including how he and the other convict, Compeyson, were on trial together. He tells us that the defence lawyer introduced Compeyson as '**well brought up**' and Magwitch as '**ill brought up**', and says that both of them will be '**spoke to**' accordingly. The court shows mercy towards Compeyson because of his good character. Magwitch, on the other hand, is sentenced to be transported to Australia.

 Explain in three or four bullet points what this says about justice in Dickens's time. Mention the significance of language and personal appearance.

 Is Dickens just writing about the criminal justice system or is he making a wider point about Victorian society? Think back to the information in Unit 3 about what people thought made a 'gentleman'.

Find out more about context and setting in the novel in Unit 12.

Watch some actors put Magwitch in the hot-seat on Cambridge Elevate.

'… he is attached to me, strongly attached to me.'

Pip: Chapter 41

GETTING IT INTO WRITING

How does Dickens present Magwitch at this point in the novel?

Now that you have worked with a range of details from the text, you need to show your skill in understanding an **interpretation**.

Look at this question:

In Chapter 39, Magwitch says, 'I lived rough, that you should live smooth.' What do you think this shows about Magwitch? Write about:

- **how Dickens presents the convict's actions in one extract from this chapter**
- **how Dickens presents the convict's actions in the novel as a whole.**

1 Use your text lasso to choose an appropriate extract. Use the following steps to help you prepare an answer:

a   Write the first line of your essay. If you have written 'In this essay I am going to …', cross it out and think of a more direct way to start – every word must earn its place in your answer.

b   When you have finished your opening paragraph, swap with a partner. Underline any words which, in your opinion, do not earn their place. If sentences do not say anything about plot, **characters**, themes or language, highlight them!

c   Swap back and discuss your marking.

d   Now use the notes from your work in this unit to write a full plan for your question (see Unit 2).

 Complete this assignment on Cambridge Elevate.

Learning checkpoint

Use your text lasso to select an extract from Chapters 39–43 that reflects the theme of ambition and self-improvement. You might want to choose a passage you have studied in this unit, such as the episode when Magwitch visits Pip in Chapter 40. Write down the chapter number, the page number, the opening sentence and closing sentence of your extract.

Using your extract, answer these questions about the theme of ambition and self-improvement:

a Explain how this extract affects Pip's knowledge about his self-improvement.

b List two or three quotations that reveal something about Pip's situation.

c Interpret these quotations, commenting on the words Dickens uses.

d Write two or three sentences linking the theme of self-improvement in your extract with the theme in the novel as a whole.

How will I know I've done this well?

✔ Comment on specific words or phrases used in the text.

✔ Explain something about the theme of self-improvement.

✔ Link the theme in your extract with at least two other places in the novel.

✔ Interrogate the language used in detail.

✔ Use accurate spelling and clear, well-punctuated sentences.

GETTING FURTHER

1 With Magwitch's return, we discover what his life was like as a young man. Write a list of bullet points about the **contrast** between Pip and Magwitch as a young man.

2 In Chapter 39, Magwitch says, '**I lived rough, that you should live smooth.**' Create a timeline showing what you think Pip and Magwitch were each doing in the years between Magwitch's arrest and his arrival in Pip's London rooms. Then write a paragraph interpreting Magwitch's rough/smooth comment.

Contexts

In the early 19th century, crime was punished severely. Prisons became overcrowded and so rotting wooden ships, called hulks, were used as additional prison space. Magwitch escapes from one of these when he first meets Pip. The punishment of 'transportation' meant that a convicted criminal would be taken to a penal (punishment) colony in Australia. Conditions were harsh and thousands died. After serving their prison sentence they were released, but they had to stay in Australia. If a convict returned to Britain, they could be hanged. Even after release, life was very harsh. There were, however, success stories – and Magwitch is one of these.

Dickens was interested in crime and punishment. As a child, he saw his father imprisoned for debt. As an adult he became interested in social reform and wanted prisons to be more humane places. He was a leading campaigner against the death penalty.

49

6

Pip's love and loyalty

How does Dickens explore relationships?

Your progress in this unit:
- explore the characters of Miss Havisham and Estella
- explore the relationships between Pip, Miss Havisham and Estella
- rewrite an extract from the point of view of Miss Havisham or Estella
- work with an editor to improve your writing.

GETTING STARTED – THE STORY AND YOU

Pip is ashamed that his rise in society has been paid for by a criminal. He is also upset that Miss Havisham allowed him to believe that she was his benefactor. What hope does he now have with Estella? He goes to Satis House to confront Miss Havisham and to see Estella.

Love and loyalty: role-play or script

Ali is desperately in love with Sam. Sam seems to show no interest in Ali and is often quite rude to her, but Ali still thinks Sam is wonderful. Ali believes that by remaining faithful and loyal, Sam will one day grow to love her. Jo is Ali's best friend. She thinks that Sam is bad for Ali. Jo is worried to see Ali so unhappy.

Either:

1 Improvise a conversation between Ali and Jo in which Jo gives Ali advice.

Or:

2 Working alone or in pairs, write out the **dialogue** between Jo and Sam as a short script of 10–15 lines. Afterwards, give the script a simple reality check: do the **characters** say anything you cannot imagine yourself saying?

GETTING CLOSER – FOCUS ON DETAILS

Read the brief summaries of Chapters 44–48 to get an overview of the section you are about to explore.

 Watch characters from the novel summarise Chapters 44–48 on Cambridge Elevate.

1 Skim Chapters 46, 47 and 48 and find a suitable quotation to accompany the summary of these chapters.

 Key terms

improvise: to make something up as you go along, with no planning.

Chapter 44

Miss Havisham admits to Pip that she led him on and Estella tells him she will marry Bentley Drummle.

'I am as unhappy as you can ever have meant me to be.'

Chapter 45

Pip meets Wemmick, who has learned that Compeyson is pursuing Magwitch.

'I came to what I did after hearing what I heard.'

Chapter 46

Pip discusses a plan for Magwitch's escape.

Chapter 47

Pip's debts pile up as he refuses to spend Magwitch's money.

Chapter 48

Pip notices that Jaggers's housekeeper, Molly, bears a strong resemblance to Estella.

Staging *Great Expectations*

Great Expectations has been adapted for film, television and theatre. Look at this example play script from Pip's visit to Satis House in Chapter 44:

The room of Satis House. There is a fire in the grate. Estella knits. Pip stands. Miss Havisham sits and watches.

Miss Havisham gradually withdraws her eyes and turns them on the fire. Estella continues to knit.

Miss H: What else?

Pip: Estella, you know I love you. You know that I have loved
           you long and dearly.

Estella raises her eyes but continues with her needlework. Miss Havisham looks between the two of them.

Pip: I should have said this sooner, but for my long mistake.
           It induced me to hope that Miss Havisham meant us
           for one another. While I thought you could not help
           yourself, as it were, I refrained from saying it.
           But I must say it now.

Estella shakes her head.

Pip: I know. I have no hope that I shall ever call you mine,
           Estella. I am ignorant what may become of me, how poor
           I may be, or where I may go. Still, I love you. I have
           loved you ever since I first saw you in this house.

Unmoved she shakes her head again.

Pip: It would have been cruel in Miss Havisham, horribly
           cruel, to practise on the susceptibility of a poor boy,
           and to torture me through all these years with a vain
           hope and an idle pursuit, if she had reflected on the
           gravity of what she did. But I think she did not. I
           think that in the endurance of her own trial, she forgot
           mine, Estella.

Miss Havisham puts her hand to her heart, looking by turns at Estella and at Pip.

Estella: It seems that there are sentiments, fancies – I
           don't know how to call them – which I am not able to
           comprehend. When you say you love me, I know what you
           mean, as a form of words; but nothing more. You address
           nothing in my breast, you touch nothing there. I don't
           care for what you say at all. I have tried to warn you
           of this; now, have I not?

```
Pip:        Yes.

Estella:    Yes. But you would not be warned, for you thought I did
            not mean it. Now, did you not think so?

Pip:        I thought and hoped you could not mean it. You, so young,
            untried, and beautiful, Estella! Surely it is not in
            Nature.

Estella:    It is in my nature. I make a great difference between you
            and all other people when I say so much. I can do no more.
```

 1 Work in groups of three. Take a different character each and perform the lines, trying to show each character's thoughts and feelings. Think about how they would say the words, their posture and movements, gestures and facial expressions.

Watch actors perform an adaptation on Cambridge Elevate.

Marking the moment

This activity allows actors to look more deeply into their characters and explore the thoughts behind their words.

1 Work in groups of four or five. Three of you perform the script while the others watch. At any point in the performance, those watching can stop the action and ask questions. Try to find out what the characters are thinking and feeling. The actors must answer in role.

2 When you have finished, work individually and make bullet-point notes of your discoveries about each character. For each of your character notes, find a quotation from the novel to support what you think.

 Watch actors carrying out a 'marking the moment' activity on Cambridge Elevate.

 Watch some of the characters speak their thoughts aloud on Cambridge Elevate.

PUTTING DETAILS TO USE

Reading the subtext

Great Expectations is full of **nuances**. Of course, you need to study what the characters say and do, but often the significance of an episode will be found in what characters do not say or do. This is called the **subtext**.

This may seem confusing – after all, if a writer has something to say, why don't they just say it? The answer is that Dickens, like all interesting artists, is creating a work of art about subtle things. If you summarised *Great Expectations* as 'social ambition messes up your relationships', you would have missed out almost all of the story. If your conclusion was that 'Pip ought to have finished his apprenticeship with Joe, married Biddy and settled down in the village', you would have missed the subtlety.

This novel has been popular for 150 years because it is multi-layered. It is amusing, but it also engages a reader's emotions and intelligence. We find ourselves wondering what the characters mean with their words. What do they want?

 Key terms

nuance: a subtle meaning or shade of meaning that is not always obvious in a text.

subtext: the unwritten part of a text – the ideas that are hidden underneath the words.

Interpreting: surface and depths

Re-read Chapter 44, which tells of Pip's visit to Satis House. Then carry out these activities to find out more about the thoughts and feelings of the three main characters.

Pip

1 a Estella retains an '**unmoved countenance**'. She gives Pip no indication that she cares about him. Why do you think he is still in love with her?

b Pip confesses his love to Estella in a very formal way. Write down a quotation as evidence of this.

c Look at how Dickens presents Pip in this scene. Do you think we are being encouraged to admire him, laugh at him or feel sorry for him? Find evidence in the text to support your views.

Estella

2 a Estella says: '**When you say you love me, I know what you mean, as a form of words; but nothing more.**' Explain what you think she means by this.

b We are now about three-quarters of the way through the novel. What information do we have about Estella so far?

c Write a paragraph explaining what you think about Estella. You might want to use some of the following words:

sympathy	frightened	young
cold	proud	lonely
selfish	cruel	poor

Miss Havisham

3 '**I saw Miss Havisham put her hand to her heart and hold it there, as she sat looking by turns at Estella and at me.**'

a In what way does this action add to or alter our understanding of Miss Havisham's character?

b How do you think Miss Havisham feels about the way she has treated Pip?

c How do you think Miss Havisham feels about the way she has treated Estella?

Narrative structure

Dickens is often called a 'master storyteller'. This means he is good at making readers want to find out:

- what is going to happen next in the text (Will Magwitch be caught? Will Estella agree to marry Pip?)
- the significance of some mystery in the subtext (What do Estella's words and silences mean? Are Pip's 'expectations' a good thing?)

1 In Chapter 47, Wopsle tells Pip that he saw a man sitting behind him at the theatre:

'I had a ridiculous fancy that he must be with you, Mr. Pip, till I saw that you were quite unconscious of him, sitting behind you there, like a ghost.'

a What three words does Wopsle use that make this incident seem chilling?

b How does this incident begin to build **narrative tension** as we approach the final part of the novel?

2 In Chapter 48, Pip realises that Molly resembles Estella:

I looked at those hands, I looked at those eyes, I looked at that flowing hair; and I compared them with other hands, other eyes, other hair, that I knew of. [...] And I felt absolutely certain that this woman was Estella's mother.

a How does this discovery add to the narrative tension?
b What does this discovery add to our understanding of Estella?

 Find out more about plot and structure in the novel in Unit 11.

3 Following the dinner with Jaggers, Pip and Wemmick walk away together and talk about Molly. During the conversation there is a single reference to her suspected ethnicity:

'... I believe had some gypsy blood in her.'

Why do you think Dickens included this passing remark? What do you think he intended to add to our understanding of both Molly and Estella?

 Key terms

narrative tension: the excitement the reader feels as they turn the page to find out what happens next in the story.

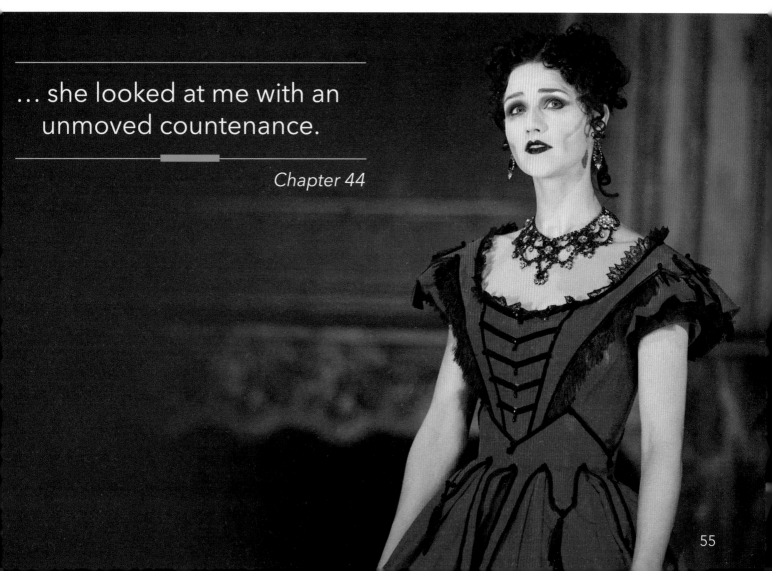

... she looked at me with an unmoved countenance.

Chapter 44

GETTING IT INTO WRITING

Writing in the first person

The novel is written using a **first-person narrator** – Pip. The response of the other characters (for example Estella and Miss Havisham in Chapter 44) is written from Pip's perspective – his understanding of the situation. Throughout the whole novel, we only really know what Pip thinks. Sometimes we like him and sometimes we don't. We may get infuriated with him. We may find his actions irritating. We may want to shout at him, 'Don't do that!'

> **Key terms**
>
> **first person:** a way of writing that tells a story through the eyes of one of the characters, using the pronouns 'I', 'my' and 'me'.

Earlier in this unit, you investigated what Miss Havisham and Estella might be thinking. You are now going to develop those ideas into creative writing.

1 Use your text lasso to choose an extract of around 300 words. This should focus on the relationships between Pip, Estella and Miss Havisham. Use the ideas and notes you have made throughout this unit to help you write your own version of the extract with **either** Miss Havisham **or** Estella as the first-person narrator.

You will need to use your knowledge and understanding of the rest of the novel to develop the character's thoughts.

2 Write a short account of the evidence on which you based your **interpretation**. What was it in the novel that made you decide Miss Havisham and Estella had those particular thoughts, feelings and motives?

They both raised their eyes as I went in, and both saw an alteration in me.

Chapter 44

3 For an extra challenge, try to write in Dickens's style. To help you with this, make a list of six or seven words and four or five phrases from your extract that you think are most typical of Dickens's style. Include them in your own version.

Working with an editor

1 Swap your version of the extract with that of another student.

a   As an editor, read through your partner's version of the extract. Write your thoughts in the margins of their work, using a different colour pen.

b   Have a meeting with your author in which you feed back some of your thoughts about their work. Authors are notoriously temperamental and moody, so you will need to be thoughtful and helpful.

c   Swap roles and allow them to comment on your piece of writing.

 Complete this assignment on Cambridge Elevate.

GETTING FURTHER

1 Dickens wrote *Great Expectations* to be published in his own magazine, so he had to write a particular number of words for each instalment. How might this have affected the style of *Great Expectations*? Discuss this in small groups.

2 Dickens also performed extracts of *Great Expectations*. In your groups, discuss which chapters from this unit would work as a dramatic reading. What qualities make it suitable for reading aloud? Would you need to cut some passages to make it work better?

3 Pip and Estella meet and he falls in love, but it takes him the rest of the novel to work out the relationship. Think about any romantic comedies you have read (or films you have seen) and discuss the parallels with *Great Expectations*. If you are studying *Romeo and Juliet*, you could use this as your text for comparison. Think about using words such as 'narrative tension', 'irony' and 'characterisation' in your answer.

 Learning checkpoint

Pip's relationship with Estella lies at the heart of the novel. Using your work so far, write a paragraph explaining Pip's feelings for Estella at this point in the story. Use supporting details from the text in your response.

7

Crime, guilt and forgiveness

What themes have developed by this point in the novel?

Your progress in this unit:
- illustrate and interrogate Miss Havisham's actions in the novel
- form ideas and perspectives about the themes of virtue, good character, love, loyalty and deceit
- prepare a case for the trial of Miss Havisham.

GETTING STARTED – THE STORY AND YOU

Pip visits Miss Havisham. She is full of remorse for how she has manipulated Estella and caused her to break Pip's heart. Pip is kind towards Miss Havisham and then goes for a walk in the ruined garden. He looks back at the house and imagines that he sees the body of Miss Havisham hanging from a beam.

Cruelty and forgiveness

Joely was going out with Ben, who was loyal but a bit boring. Eventually she found him so dull she dumped him (via Facebook). Afterwards Ben started going out with Natalie. Joely was jealous and worked out a plan with Gloria. Gloria would tempt Ben away from Natalie.

Ben fell for Gloria and dumped Natalie (via Facebook). Gloria posted publicly, asking Ben to meet her in town on Tuesday. When he got there, Gloria was waiting … with Natalie, Joely and half the girls in Year 10. Everyone laughed at Ben. Loads of people took photos and posted them on Facebook that evening.

The next day, everyone in school knew what had happened. They teased Ben so much he ran out of his English class. But when Joely heard about this she felt terrible. She wrote angry messages to her friends, telling them to leave Ben alone. She said that she really loved Ben, that she was sorry and wanted to get back together with him.

1 Work in groups. Discuss Ben's dilemma. How do you think he should react? What should he reply to Joely?

2 In what ways does this scenario mirror the events in *Great Expectations*?

GETTING CLOSER – FOCUS ON DETAILS

Read through the brief summaries of Chapters 49–53 to get an overview of the section you are about to explore.

 Watch characters from the novel summarise Chapters 49–53 on Cambridge Elevate.

1 Look at the following quotations and match each one to a chapter in the chart.

a   He flared the candle at me again, smoking my face and hair, and for an instant blinding me.

b   'Believe this: when she first came, I meant to save her from misery like mine.'

c   Towards the marshes I now went straight, having no time to spare.

d   'I know I am quite myself. And the man we have in hiding down the river, is Estella's Father.'

e   'Put the case that at the same time he held a trust to find a child for an eccentric rich lady to adopt and bring up.'

Choosing a key event

1 Re-read Chapter 49. Decide which you think is the key event in the chapter. Narrow that down to one key quotation and use your text lasso to choose an extract of around 300 words that includes the quotation. Answer the following questions about your chosen extract.

a   Choose three words or phrases from your extract and analyse what makes each one dramatic.

b   How does Dickens create the mood and tone of your extract? Look closely at the language and structure.

c   Think about the narrative structure – the order in which the story has been told. Why has Dickens chosen to put this incident towards the end of the **novel**?

Chapter 49
Miss Havisham apologises to Pip but as he leaves, she sets herself on fire.

Chapter 50
Pip finds out that Magwitch is Estella's father.

Chapter 51
Jaggers admits that Molly is Estella's mother, but says he had not realised that Magwitch was her father.

Chapter 52
Pip receives a letter regarding 'Uncle Provis'. It asks Pip to meet secretly in the marshes.

Chapter 53
Orlick confesses that he murdered Pip's sister and admits an association with the convict Compeyson.

PUTTING DETAILS TO USE

The following tasks will help you understand the **characters** in more depth.

Character and characterisation

1 Read the following statements and decide whether you agree or disagree with them.

a   Miss Havisham has abused Pip; she should not be forgiven.

b   Miss Havisham has suffered much in her life; we should understand this and not be too harsh on her.

c   Pip could have walked away from the situation at any time; he did not need to visit Satis House.

d   Miss Havisham is a confused old lady and cannot be held accountable for her actions.

e   The fault lies with society and its institutions, which have allowed someone like Miss Havisham to be Estella's guardian.

Language and narrative

1 At the end of Chapter 49, Pip sees Miss Havisham on fire:

> I saw a great flaming light spring up. In the same moment, I saw her running at me, shrieking, with a whirl of fire blazing all about her, and soaring at least as many feet above her head as she was high.

a   Write down the verbs that Dickens uses. What do you notice about them?

b   Does Dickens's account make you think that this was an accident or a deliberate act?

2 'Take the pencil and write under my name, – "I forgive her".' Do you think Pip forgives Miss Havisham? Write a paragraph giving the reasons for your answer.

… a whirl of fire blazing all about her.

Chapter 49

Mysteries explained

At the beginning of Chapter 50, Herbert tells Pip the story of the young woman and Provis's/Magwitch's child. He is **reporting** the story.

'… the young woman presented herself before Provis for one moment, and swore that she would destroy the child (which was in her possession), and he should never see it again; then, she vanished. – There's the worst arm comfortably in the sling.'

1 Write down three reasons why Dickens chose to reveal this information near the end of the story.

We find out about Estella's father in a rather complicated way:

Pip is the book's **narrator**, but here he reports a story he hears from **Herbert**, who in turn reports a tale told by **Magwitch**.

The story of Estella's mother was also complicated. In Chapter 48, we read:

Pip's account of **Wemmick**'s story of **Jaggers**'s defence of **Molly**, which he knows about perhaps from Jaggers himself or perhaps from the gossip of other lawyers.

2 Look at how Pip asks questions in these two scenes. His investigation makes this part of the book read a bit like a detective story.

a   List the crimes that occur, are recalled or are mentioned (whether actually carried out or not) in the book. Think about the different things that Magwitch, Molly, Compeyson and Orlick either do or pretend to do. Some of their actions are clearly stated but others are only implied.

b   Write a paragraph about the importance of secrecy and deception in the plot.

In Chapter 51, Pip goes to Jaggers's office and tells him that he knows about Provis/Magwitch:

'So! You know the young lady's father, Pip?' said Mr. Jaggers.
'Yes,' I replied, 'and his name is Provis – from New South Wales.'
Even Mr. Jaggers started when I said those words. It was the slightest start that could escape a man, the most carefully repressed and the soonest checked, but he did start, though he made it a part of the action of taking out his pocket-handkerchief.

3 Look carefully at the language Dickens uses in this extract.

a   List four words that describe how Jaggers tries to hide his reaction (e.g. '**slightest**').

b   Comment on the impression Dickens's use of language makes on the reader.

c   Why is this a significant moment in their relationship? Think about who knows what and who is challenging whom.

 Learning checkpoint

a   Describe, with supporting details, how Pip's **character** has changed by this point in the **novel**.

b   Describe, with supporting details, the significance of the fire in the setting of Satis House.

c   Describe some of the strong **feelings and attitudes** shown by Miss Havisham, Pip and Mr Jaggers.

d   Choose one quotation and explain how it has helped you to **interpret** a character or event.

GETTING IT INTO WRITING

Themes: guilt and innocence

The story in *Great Expectations* is driven by various crimes and their consequences. However, the **theme** of wrongdoing is wider than this. In Chapter 49, Miss Havisham reflects on her own guilt, saying three things over and over again:

'What have I done!'

'When she first came, I meant to save her from misery like mine.'

'Take the pencil and write under my name, "I forgive her!"'

1 Using an extract (300–350 words) of your choice from Chapter 49, explain and explore Miss Havisham's feelings. Write about:

a how Dickens presents Miss Havisham's feelings in the extract

b how Dickens presents her feelings in the novel as a whole.

Note that for this question you will need to gather and **interpret** evidence.

2 Now re-read the scene in which Miss Havisham asks for Pip's forgiveness and then answer the following question:

In what ways is forgiveness a key theme in *Great Expectations*?

Consider what role forgiveness plays in the plot. There are several scenes in which different characters offer forgiveness or ask to be forgiven – Pip himself does both. Think also about the characters in the novel who have been wronged and consider how **not forgiving** is part of the theme.

 Complete this assignment on Cambridge Elevate.

GETTING FURTHER

Lawyers' chambers and law courts are important **settings** in Great Expectations. For this activity, you are going to put Miss Havisham on trial. You will need people to play the parts of:

- Miss Havisham
- the prosecuting lawyer(s)
- Miss Havisham's defence lawyer(s)
- witnesses (e.g. Pip, Estella, Jaggers)
- the judge
- the jury.

The prosecution

As the prosecuting lawyer, your aim is to convince the jury of Miss Havisham's guilt. While preparing the case for the prosecution, consider these points:

- As her guardian, Miss Havisham should have Estella's best interests at heart, but instead she uses Estella to her own ends.
- She encourages Estella to cause men pain and anguish as a way of getting her own revenge on them.
- She singles out Pip – a young and entirely innocent boy – and knowingly manipulates his life so that he will suffer heartbreak.
- She takes away Estella's childhood from her.
- She allows Pip to think that she is the secret benefactor.

You will need to back up all these points from the text. Who will you call as witnesses?

 Watch a case for the prosecution being prepared on Cambridge Elevate.

The defence

As a defence lawyer, you will need to work with Miss Havisham to prepare her case. Do you want to plead that she is completely innocent or that, though guilty, there are 'mitigating circumstances', which means that when they know the background to her actions, the jury will be more sympathetic. Consider these points when preparing your case:

- Miss Havisham provided for Estella: she was housed, clothed, fed and educated.
- Estella never had to go out to work.
- Without Miss Havisham, Estella might have died or faced a life of poverty.
- This was a time when many children had to grow up quickly, so Estella is not unusual in missing her childhood.
- Child abuse was not recognised by her culture and society.
- Miss Havisham asks for forgiveness at the end.
- Miss Havisham suffered great hurt herself and never recovered from the shock of it.

Remember to find evidence from the text to support your claims. Who will you call as witnesses?

 Watch a case for the defence being prepared on Cambridge Elevate.

 Watch the trial of Miss Havisham on Cambridge Elevate.

The trial

Follow the order of events in the chart. Throughout the trial, the judge keeps order and directs proceedings.

The judge introduces the case.

↓

The prosecution puts forward the case against Miss Havisham.

↓

The defence puts forward the defence of Miss Havisham.

↓

The prosecution calls witnesses for questioning, probably starting with Miss Havisham.

↓

The defence questions the prosecution witnesses and then calls their own.

↓

The prosecution sums up their case.

↓

The defence sums up their case.

↓

The jury retires to discuss their verdict. They elect a foreman (spokesperson).

↓

The court returns and the foreman of the jury gives the verdict.

8

Escape!

How does Dickens make his novel so dramatic?

Your progress in this unit:

- present a dramatic reading
- examine the methods Dickens uses to make his writing dramatic
- undertake a writing task in timed conditions.

GETTING STARTED – THE STORY AND YOU

It is the morning of the escape. Pip, Herbert, Startop and Magwitch head out in a rowing boat. They aim to get Magwitch on to a steamer to Hamburg. However, they are followed by a much larger rowing boat. No matter how hard they row, they are unable to stop the galley from gaining on them.

Writing a chase narrative

1 Write a short story (roughly 100 words) about a chase. It could be in a modern **setting** using cars, or it could take place in a different era using another form of transport for the pursuit, such as horses. When you have finished, read your piece aloud to a partner. Make your reading as dramatic and exciting as possible.

2 When you have heard your partner's story, discuss your readings. What did you do to make your reading dramatic? Make a bullet-point list of five techniques. For example did you speed up certain parts of the story or say some parts softly and mysteriously?

GETTING CLOSER - FOCUS ON DETAILS

Charting the progress

 1 Create your own chart for Chapters 54–56 based on the charts in the previous units. Give each chapter a one-sentence summary and a key quotation. If you can, add to your chart by finding pictures that go with each chapter.

> **Watch characters from the novel summarise Chapters 54–56 on Cambridge Elevate.**

Preparing a dramatic reading

1 You are going to prepare a dramatic reading. Use your text lasso to choose an exciting extract from Chapter 54. To help you prepare, read your extract and underline six key verbs and six key phrases. Choose the ones that you find most noticeable and interesting. For example:

> It was but for an instant that I seemed to struggle with a thousand mill-weirs and a thousand flashes of light; that instant past, I was taken on board the galley.

2 Annotate your extract with at least five instructions that will make your reading dramatic. For example:

- *point to the audience*
- *make a gesture with right hand*
- *shout*
- *whisper*
- *read in a ferocious manner.*

 > **Watch an actor prepare a dramatic reading on Cambridge Elevate.**

3 Now work with a partner, who will be your director. Present your dramatic reading to them. It is the director's job to stop you and make suggestions for improvement. Afterwards, swap roles. As you work, consider the following:

- the pace of your reading
- the expressions you use
- using different voices for different characters
- adding simple mannerisms or gestures
- conveying emotion
- using pauses for effect
- projecting – speaking from the chest and not the throat
- enunciating – saying the beginnings and endings of words clearly.

Practise your reading at least five times in preparation for performing it to others.

4 Now deliver your dramatic reading to the class. Remember:

- Don't worry if you make a mistake. Pause and go back to the phrase you stumbled over.
- Don't be afraid of being afraid. Everyone is frightened of standing up in front of other people.
- If you can, photocopy your extract into large print.
- Refer to the words and phrases you have highlighted.
- Make sure you look up during the reading and make eye contact with your audience.
- Have fun – if you are enjoying yourself your audience will be able to tell and will pick up on your enthusiasm.

PUTTING DETAILS TO USE

Narrative technique and language

Dickens wanted his **novels** to be exciting. We can see this in Chapter 54, where Magwitch becomes a hunted man and fears for his life. One technique Dickens uses in this part of the novel is pointing out place names. The first lists the places Magwitch will visit during the escape that Pip and Herbert have planned. The second details the London landmarks they are passing in the boat. These lists root the events in a recognisable reality – a world with place names that readers would be familiar with. The escape may be a dramatic adventure, but it demands a series of precise, planned steps.

1 Dickens uses several other techniques in this episode to build dramatic tension. Find three quotations that show how Dickens makes this event tense and dramatic. For example:

> The night was as dark by this time as it would be by morning; and what light we had, seemed to come more from the river than the sky, as the oars in their dipping struck at a few reflected stars.

2 Find three examples of repetition in Dickens's description of the galley finally catching up with the escapees. Explain the effect of this technique.

3 The two ex-convicts struggle in the water and both disappear:

> … every man looking silently and eagerly at the water astern. Presently a dark object was seen in it, bearing towards us on the tide. No man spoke, but the steersman held up his hand, and all softly backed water, and kept the boat straight and true before it.

Write down three ways in which Dickens creates tension in this quotation. For example:

The men do not speak to each other; this suggests they are afraid that both Magwitch and Compeyson have drowned.

4 Dickens chooses a very dramatic setting for these events. Make a list of the danger that the setting creates. For example:

These events take place on the water. This creates a sense of danger because we know that any fight may end with someone drowning.

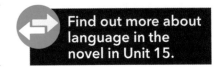 **Find out more about language in the novel in Unit 15.**

Understanding pathos

These chapters also contain points of **pathos**. At the end of Chapter 54, for example, after Magwitch's injury and capture, Magwitch advises Pip to leave:

'It's best as a gentleman should not be knowed to belong to me now.'

1 Make notes on what Magwitch's advice tells us about:

a   his relationship with Pip
b   the concept of 'gentleman'.

However, Pip replies:

'I will never stir from your side,' said I, 'when I am suffered to be near you. Please God, I will be as true to you as you have been to me!'

2 Write notes on what Pip's reply tells us about:

a   his development as a person
b   his relationship with Magwitch.

Contexts

Dickens loved the theatre. As a young man, he wanted to be an actor and aged 20 he was invited to audition for a play. However, the night before the audition he came down with a cold and could not speak, so he missed the audition. After this, his career as a journalist took off and he never went back to acting. He maintained a love of performing, though, and he wrote several plays and carried out public readings of his novels. He played all the characters with different voices and managed to communicate great excitement in the narrative.

When he performed, Dickens stood on a stage behind a wine-coloured table and wore white gloves. His scripts are annotated with directions such as, 'snap fingers' or speak with 'terror till the end!' Famously, after seeing him perform a reading of the death of Nancy in *Oliver Twist*, his friend John Foster asked him to stop such ferocious performance in case he drove himself to an early grave!

Key terms

pathos: from the Greek word meaning 'suffering', this is an appeal to the reader's emotions, particularly passages likely to cause pity and sorrow.

… what light we had, seemed to come more from the river than the sky.

Chapter 54

Narrative and character

In Chapter 56, Magwitch lies ill. Pip remains loyal to him and visits him in prison:

A smile crossed his face then, he turned his eyes on me with a trustful look, as if he were confident that I had seen some small redeeming touch in him, even so long ago as when I was a little child. As to all the rest, he was humble and contrite, and I never knew him complain.

1 Think about the development of Pip and Magwitch's relationship during the novel. Summarise each stage of their relationship in a bullet point. For example:

- When Pip first meets Magwitch, the convict seizes him and threatens to kill him.
- The second time they meet …

When Magwitch has been condemned to death, Pip pays him another visit:

'It is just the time,' said I. 'I waited for it at the gate.'
'You always waits at the gate; don't you, dear boy?'
'Yes. Not to lose a moment of the time.'
'Thank'ee dear boy, thank'ee. God bless you! You've never deserted me, dear boy.'
I pressed his hand in silence, for I could not forget that I had once meant to desert him.

2 Write two bullet points explaining what the language tells us about Pip's attitude to Magwitch at this point in the story.

3 One of the **themes** in this novel is Pip's developing character as his circumstances change and events affect him. What does this episode tell us about Pip?

The descriptions of Magwitch emphasise his physical suffering:

'Are you in much pain to-day?'
'I don't complain of none, dear boy.'
'You never do complain.'

4 Why do you think Magwitch doesn't complain?

Secrets and lies

Just before Magwitch dies at the end of Chapter 56, Pip tells him that he has a daughter:

'Dear Magwitch, I must tell you, now at last. You understand what I say?'
A gentle pressure on my hand.
'You had a child once, whom you loved and lost.'
A stronger pressure on my hand.
'She lived and found powerful friends. She is living now. She is a lady and very beautiful. And I love her!'

1 Why do you think Pip wants to tell Magwitch this now when he has kept it secret for so long?

2 List other examples in the novel of people keeping secrets, lying or being deceitful in other ways. Jaggers is an obvious example, but there are many others. Write down:

a   who they are
b   what the secret or deception is
c   who they are deceiving
d   their motives or reasons.

... he turned his eyes on me with a trustful look.

Chapter 56

GETTING IT INTO WRITING

Writing under timed conditions

You will be expected to spend approximately 50 minutes on the *Great Expectations* section of your English Literature exam. You will be given an extract from the novel to write about, but your writing should also demonstrate your understanding of the whole novel. Look at this question:

Charles Dickens: *Great Expectations*

[*In the exam you will be provided with the extract of around 300–350 words but for this exercise use the extract you have found and studied in the unit.*]

Choose an extract from Chapter 54 and write about:

- **How Dickens makes the escape exciting and dramatic**
- **How Dickens makes other events in the novel exciting and dramatic.**

[30 marks]

---

1 Answer this question in 50 minutes. Writing under pressure can be difficult, so it is important to practise. Use these tips to help you:

- Have a countdown clock nearby to keep an eye on the time.
- Underline the key words in the task.
- Take a few minutes to produce a spider diagram of your ideas.
- Quickly sketch out an opening and closing sentence.
- Remember to use three or four quotations.
- Allow yourself a few minutes to check your writing at the end.

 Complete this assignment on Cambridge Elevate.

 Learning checkpoint

Use your text lasso to choose a 300-word extract that includes some part of the attempted escape. Write down the chapter number, the page number, and the opening and closing sentences of your extract. Using your extract, write two or three sentences for each of the following:

a Explain why you think your extract illustrates the escape.

b Write down two or three quotations that illustrate the language used to create the tension in the escape.

c Examine the words used in the quotations and explain why you think Dickens has used them.

d Explain why you think Dickens has included this section at this moment in the story.

GETTING FURTHER

In Chapter 55, while the arrested Magwitch is lying in prison, Wemmick explains how Compeyson found out about the escape attempt. He asks Pip to forgive him. The two men go for a walk and end up at a church, where Wemmick says: '**Halloa! … Here's Miss Skiffins! Let's have a wedding.**' The light comedy of this episode **contrasts** strikingly with the dark drama of life and death that comes immediately before and after it.

1   a   Why do you think Dickens chose to put this event here?

     b   What does it tell you about the structure of the novel as a whole?

When planning your answer, think about the fact that:

- Wemmick himself (and his apology) form a link between the two storylines
- contrast is a noticeable aspect of the structure of the novel in several other places.

Magwitch is tried, found guilty and sentenced to death. Dickens does not leave the matter there, though – Magwitch is just one of a crowd of convicted people:

But for the indelible picture that my remembrance now holds before me, I could scarcely believe, even as I write these words, that I saw two-and-thirty men and women put before the Judge to receive that sentence together.

2   Why does Dickens tell us the number of people condemned to death that day?

I saw two-and-thirty men and women put before the Judge to receive that sentence together.

Chapter 55

9

Maturity and true friendship

How does Dickens bring events to a climax?

Your progress in this unit:
- examine the friendship between Pip and Joe
- chart the theme of friendship in the novel as a whole
- try an 'open book' writing task.

GETTING STARTED – THE STORY AND YOU

With Magwitch no longer there to support him, Pip's debts spiral out of control. He falls into a decline and becomes terribly ill.

Opportunity knocks

Joolz was going to the top. His older brother Jim had long since got used to telling people 'my brother's the clever one'. When the letter came to say he had passed the scholarship exams, Jim said: 'Some people pass exams, some people don't'. Joolz went off to boarding school; Jim was already at the local town school.

Joolz did well. He won awards at school, then went to work as a banker in the City. He dressed more and more smartly and his accent changed. He made a lot of money. But then his luck ran out. His bank came under investigation and he became very ill. His brother Jim took charge – he went to collect Joolz from the hospital and brought him home. Joolz began to depend on Jim for everything.

1 All relationships can be affected by different levels of success or status – such as the differences that open up between Pip and Joe in *Great Expectations*.

 a What is your experience of school opportunities? Do you feel things work out fairly?

 b There are several different types of schools, including academies, high schools, grammar schools, fee-paying schools and faith schools. In groups, discuss what you think are the implications of these different approaches. Do they create different opportunities? Is there real choice? Do the different opportunities make the system an unfair one?

GETTING CLOSER – FOCUS ON DETAILS

Read through the summaries and quotations from Chapters 57 and 58 to get an overview of the section you are about to explore.

 Watch characters from the novel summarise Chapters 57 and 58 on Cambridge Elevate.

Understanding Joe Gargery

In this unit, we are going to concentrate on Joe Gargery. Hold a **dialectic** to investigate the **character** of Joe.

1 Work with another student. One of you is **A** and one is **B**. **A** will argue that Joe is a good and loyal friend. **B** will argue that Joe is weak, stupid and easily used by others.

Place two chairs opposite each other. Your argument should take place in two rounds of two minutes each. **A** will make the first argument and then **B** will reply with a counter-argument. Speak respectfully and listen to your opponent before replying. When preparing your arguments, consider the following points.

A: Joe is a good and loyal friend:

- He seems to have the simple and straightforward values that might be appropriate for a blacksmith.
- He is reflective and listens to Pip.
- Sometimes he says wise things.
- He is kind.
- He does not stand in Pip's way when Pip decides to go to London.
- He looks after Pip when Pip is ill.

B: Joe is weak, stupid and easily used by others:

- He does not protect Pip from Mrs Joe's beatings.
- He does not prevent Pip going to Miss Havisham.
- He employs Orlick, who ends up murdering Mrs Joe.
- He does not stop Pip going to London to live with strangers.
- He forgives Pip without knowing what he is forgiving.

Chapter 57

Pip is nursed back to health by Joe. When he recovers he decides to propose to Biddy.

Joe had actually laid his head down on the pillow at my side and put his arm round my neck, in his joy that I knew him.

Chapter 58

On returning to his home on the marshes, Pip learns that Joe and Biddy are married. He decides to accept Herbert's invitation to go to Cairo and work as a clerk.

'Dear Joe, I hope you will have children to love.'

Themes and character

Unlike so many of the characters in the **novel**, Dickens presents Joe as honest and uncomplicated. He holds the simple values that you might expect from someone in a traditional job, living in a traditional village in the 19th century. He is also reflective and listens to Pip, and he is often wise. When Pip confesses that his account of his first visit to Miss Havisham's was entirely made up, Joe is faced with issues of morality and also motivation:

'… lies is lies. Howsever they come, they didn't ought to come, and they come from the father of lies, and work round to the same. Don't you tell no more of 'em, Pip. That ain't the way to get out of being common, old chap.'

1 a Who is the 'father of lies'?
  b Joe explains his wise ideas in confused language. Write down what you think Joe means, using clear, straightforward language.
  c How does Dickens use language to **characterise** Joe in this conversation?

From the moment Pip leaves for London, a gap develops between the two men. This grows wider as Pip becomes a gentleman:

'Us two being now alone, Sir,' – began Joe.
'Joe,' I interrupted, pettishly, 'how can you call me Sir?'
Joe looked at me for a single instant with something faintly like reproach. Utterly preposterous as his cravat was, and as his collars were, I was conscious of a sort of dignity in the look.

Joe's language and his simple actions make him a comic character. Some critics argue that we are never quite sure if Dickens deliberately sets Joe up to be laughed at.

2 Write notes about the following words, explaining what they mean and what they contribute to our understanding of Joe and Pip:

  a **sir**
  b **pettishly**
  c **reproach**
  d **preposterous**
  e **dignity**.

3 Ideas about Joe's character have varied greatly in different adaptations of *Great Expectations*. He has been shown as:

  a bumbling and comical, sometimes boyish
  b quiet and thoughtful
  c good-hearted but nervous and meek, with a low opinion of his own status in the world
  d carrying the weight of the world on his shoulders.

Which of these versions comes closest to your own understanding of the character? In what way?

4 Some people think that Joe's character is too simplistic and not developed well enough to be believable. What do you think?

 Watch actors discuss Joe's character on Cambridge Elevate.

Utterly preposterous as his cravat was,
and as his collars were, I was conscious
of a sort of dignity in the look.

Chapter 27

PUTTING DETAILS TO USE

Language and character

In Chapter 57, Pip falls ill. This is a turning point in the development of his character in the novel. He becomes delirious:

That I sometimes struggled with real people, in the belief that they were murderers, and that I would all at once comprehend that they meant to do me good, and would then sink exhausted in their arms, and suffer them to lay me down, I also knew at the time.

1 How does Dickens use language (including punctuation) to portray Pip's state of mind in this extract?

2 During his illness, Pip hallucinates. List the images he sees and relate them to the things that have happened to him. In some cases the link is obvious; in others it is harder to interpret.

3 Pip describes hearing Joe as a '**home-voice**'. Write down two or three bullet points to explain the significance of this for his relationship with Joe, and for his own development. For example:

Joe has a distinctive way of speaking and Pip recognises it.

Joe's way of speaking is unmistakable. Look at these three examples:

'Which it air, old chap.'

'Which dear old Pip, old chap … you and me was ever friends. And when you're well enough to go out for a ride – what larks!'

'Which you meantersay, Pip, how long have your illness lasted, dear old chap?'

4 a Each of these statements is a reply to something that Pip has said. Read them in the **context** of Chapter 57 and then rewrite them in modern English as responses to what Pip has said in each case.

b Each of these three examples begins with the word 'which'. Write a short paragraph commenting on the grammar of Joe's language (the way he puts words together to create meaning).

 Find out more about character and characterisation in the novel in Unit 13.

Narrative structure

At the very end of Chapter 57, Pip decides to ask Biddy to marry him. He plans a whole speech that he will deliver to persuade her. It ends:

'And now, dear Biddy, if you can tell me that you will go through the world with me, you will surely make it a better world for me, and me a better man for it, and I will try hard to make it a better world for you.'

1 Write two or three sentences giving advice to Pip. Begin:

You seem not to be thinking reasonably, Pip. Have you considered Biddy in all of this?

In fact, Pip never makes the speech he has rehearsed because he discovers that Biddy is already married:

'But dear Biddy, how smart you are!'
'Yes, dear Pip.'
'And Joe, how smart you are!'
'Yes, dear old Pip, old chap.'
I looked at both of them, from one to the other, and then –
'It's my wedding-day,' cried Biddy, in a burst of happiness, 'and I am married to Joe!'

2 Think about the structuring of this news. How does Dickens place it in the novel to make it dramatic?

Towards the end of Chapter 58, Pip asks for Joe's and Biddy's forgiveness:

'And now, though I know you have already done it in your own kind hearts, pray tell me, both, that you forgive me! Pray let me hear you say the words, that I may carry the sound of them away with me, and then I shall be able to believe that you can trust me, and think better of me, in the time to come!'

3 a For what do you think Pip is asking their forgiveness?

b Do you think he is right to ask this? Why?

4 **Contrast** the way that Pip and Joe speak. What does Dickens's use of language tell us about their characters and their attitudes to the relationship?

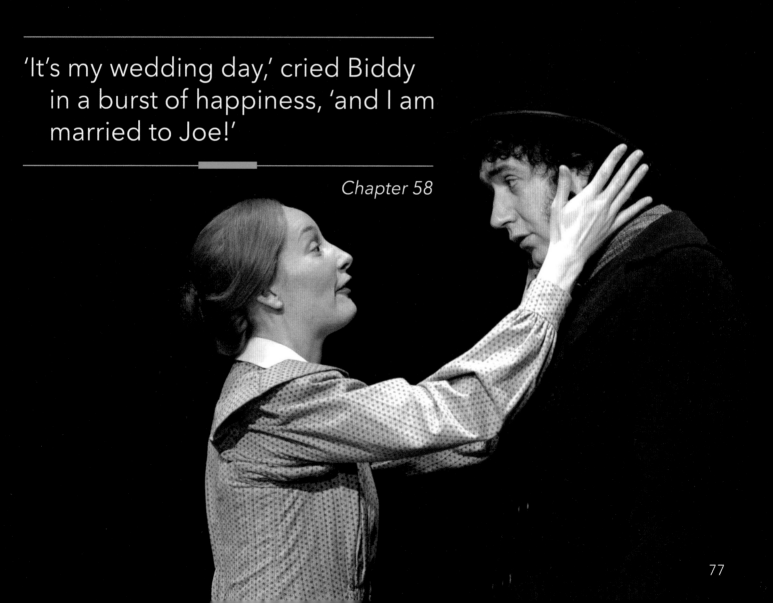

'It's my wedding day,' cried Biddy in a burst of happiness, 'and I am married to Joe!'

Chapter 58

GETTING IT INTO WRITING

Loyalty and friendship

Throughout the previous units, you have investigated several specific episodes from *Great Expectations*. However, it is important to consider the novel as a whole rather than as a series of incidents. This activity looks at the **theme** of loyalty and friendship.

Find out more about themes and ideas in the novel in Unit 14.

1 Use your text lasso to choose an extract from Chapter 57, then answer this question. Remember, in the exam an extract will be provided for you.

Loyalty and friendship are very important themes in the novel. Starting with this extract from Chapter 57, explore how Dickens presents this theme. Write about:

- **Joe's friendship and loyalty in the extract**
- **how friendship and loyalty are shown by other characters in the novel as a whole.**

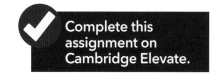

Complete this assignment on Cambridge Elevate.

2 Copy and complete the following table to further investigate the theme of friendship and loyalty.

Friendship and loyalty	Example	Key quotation
Joe and Pip	Joe releases Pip from his apprenticeship so that he can go to London.	'Pip is that harty welcome,' said Joe, 'to go free with his services, to honour and fortune, as no words can tell him.' (Chapter 18)
	Joe comes to Pip's aid when he is seriously ill in London.	At last, one day, I took courage, and said, 'Is it Joe?' And the dear old home-voice answered, 'Which it air, old chap.' (Chapter 57)
Pip and Estella		
Pip and Miss Havisham		
Pip and Herbert Pocket	Pip sets Herbert up in business without telling him. (Chapter 37)	
Pip and Magwitch	Pip cares for Magwitch when he is dying. (Chapter 56)	
Joe and Biddy		

3 What are the opposites of friendship and loyalty? What examples of these can you find in the novel?

Learning checkpoint

It is important that you can use details to show understanding and **interpretation**. Practise this skill by writing two or three paragraphs about Pip and Joe's friendship in the novel as a whole.

How will I know I've done this well?

✔ Show understanding of feelings and attitudes by describing the way that Pip's feelings change as he grows older, while Joe has been a true friend all along.

✔ Show understanding of character by describing how Pip grows up in his attitude towards Joe.

✔ Develop interpretation by writing one sentence about a quotation that helped you form an opinion of either Joe or Pip's character in these chapters of the novel.

✔ Comment on specific words or phrases used in the novel.

✔ Show how the theme is explored in different parts of the novel.

✔ Use accurate spelling and clear, well-punctuated sentences.

GETTING FURTHER

In *Great Expectations*, Joe and Mrs Joe are responsible for Pip, as his parents are dead. But although they act as his parents, Mrs Joe is of course his sister and so Joe is his brother-in-law.

1 What effect do the events of Chapters 57 and 58 have on your view of the relationships between Pip, Biddy, Joe and Mrs Joe? Write about:

- Joe taking care of Pip
- Pip intending to propose to Biddy, only to discover that Joe has already done so.

2 Friendship is an important part of several 19th-century novels. What recent films or novels do you know in which friendship and loyalty are a key theme as they are in *Great Expectations*? How are the themes represented in these other books?

... the dear old home-voice answered.

Chapter 57

How does it end?

How does Dickens tie up the loose ends?

Your progress in this unit:
- consider the ending of the novel
- examine other possible endings to the story, including another written by Dickens
- write about the ending of the novel under timed conditions.

GETTING STARTED – THE STORY AND YOU

Eleven years later, Pip comes back to visit Joe and Biddy. Now that he is making his own way in the world he seems more content. Joe and Biddy have a child. He tells Biddy that he does not think he will ever marry. In the dim, wintry afternoon Pip walks to where Satis House once stood. He finds that Estella has also come back to visit the house.

A happy ending

1 Work in groups of three or four. You are a group of screenwriters. You have been called to a meeting to sort out the plot for a film called *Ahmed and Abi*. The producers have the elements of the story but need some help working out the narrative. So far the plot has these key points:

- The film starts in a secondary school.
- Ahmed is a tough, cool guy who plays guitar.
- Abi is a clever, popular girl who plays Grade 7 piano.

- They have hated each other since Year 5, when Ahmed turned up his amp to full volume while accompanying Abi as she played 'Silent Night' in the nativity play.
- At the Year 11 school dance, Abi is due to sing a song, accompanying herself on the piano.
- Nervous on the night, Abi sings out of tune and then falls silent on stage with the whole year staring at her.
- Suddenly Ahmed appears with his lead guitar and breaks into an amazing solo. Abi finds her note, her confidence returns and they end the song together. Everyone cheers.
- The next day, Abi is due to head off to begin …

a In groups, work out seven more turning points in the plot, to reach the end. The last one should be set 10 years later. Prepare your plot for presentation at the next production meeting.

b Share your plot with others in the class and discuss the similarities and differences.

c In most films and **novels**, the ending ties up all the loose ends in the story. Did you make the ending neat and tidy? Did you give your viewers a happy ending?

GETTING CLOSER – FOCUS ON DETAILS

Investigating the ending

 1 In your scriptwriting groups, discuss Chapter 59 and compare it to the ending of your movie.

   a In what ways do you feel Dickens gives readers the ending they expect?

   b Is it an ending with a resolution?

   c Do things seem to be neatly tied up or are there problems and questions left hanging?

2 Using the internet, find an image that you feel best illustrates Chapter 59 of *Great Expectations* and the end of the novel. Write two or three sentences giving the reasons for your choice. Back up your writing with evidence from the text.

> **Watch characters from the novel summarise Chapter 59 on Cambridge Elevate.**

I took her hand in mine, and we went out of the ruined place.

Chapter 59

PUTTING DETAILS TO USE

Language and ideas

1 Study the language Dickens uses in Chapter 59 to describe the grounds of Satis House.

  a Make a list of the images. For example: '**A cold, shivery mist had veiled the afternoon**'.

  b What is the overall effect of the images?

2 Work in small groups. Discuss why you think Dickens chose to set the last chapter at Satis House. You might consider the role of this **setting** in Pip's childhood (narrative), and the fact that it is now a ruin (**symbolism**).

3 There are several references to light and the moon in this final chapter, including in the final sentence of the book. Why do you think Dickens makes these references?

To answer this question you need to know and **understand** the novel, but you also need to **interpret** the evidence. So you are likely to write about:

  • the timing and setting of the scene
  • the connections between the end of the novel with its beginning.

Estella has not appeared in the book for some time, but she has not been forgotten. She is in Pip's thoughts (e.g. when he takes care of Magwitch and when held captive by Orlick). She also appears in his conversation (e.g. in **dialogue** with Jaggers and when Joe tells Pip about Miss Havisham's will).

However, this is the first time Pip and Estella have met since he visited Satis House in Chapter 44. In narrative time, this is 11 years, which is nearly as long as Pip's life between Chapter 1 and Chapter 58. In reading time, this is 15 chapters, or about one-fifth of the novel.

4 Time has passed, but has Estella changed? Find and write out two quotations that suggest she has.

5 **a** What is the meaning of Estella's declaration '**I am greatly changed**'?

  b How does it affect the way we read the ending of the novel?

6 A great deal goes unsaid in the meeting between Pip and Estella, meaning that there is a lot for the reader to interpret.

  a Write a set of bullets summarising and commenting on:
   • what Pip says to Estella
   • what Estella says to Pip.

  b Write two short paragraphs explaining what you think:
   • Pip does not say to Estella
   • Estella does not say to Pip.

Narrative structure: the ending

In the final few paragraphs, Dickens's language is complex and sometimes difficult for a reader to understand. Look at the following examples and answer the questions about each one.

'I little thought,' said Estella, 'that I should take leave of you in taking leave of this spot. I am very glad to do so.'

---

1 What do you think Estella means by this?

I took her hand in mine and we went out of the ruined place.

---

2 **a** What do you think Pip means by this action?

  b What do you think Estella understands by this action?

... the evening mists were rising now.

Chapter 59

... as the morning mists had risen long ago when I first left the forge, so the evening mists were rising now.

3 a To what is the **narrator** referring in this extract?

b How would you interpret Dickens (and Pip) making this reference at this point?

... and in all the broad expanse of tranquil light they showed to me, I saw the shadow of no parting from her.

4 The first edition of *Great Expectations* was published with this exact ending. In later editions, Dickens revised the end of the

final sentence to read '... I saw no shadow of another parting from her.' Today, some editions of the novel use the first ending; other editions use the second one.

a What difference do you think there is in each version of this final sentence?

b Do you think it is a happy or a sad ending? Explain the reasons for your answer.

 Key terms

symbolism: the use of words or images to suggest an idea or emotion.

A selection of endings

Films usually offer endings that resolve everything. *Great Expectations* gives filmmakers great **characters**, settings and atmosphere, but the plot does not follow a classic narrative structure and the ending is unresolved.

1 Watch the endings to three different film versions of the novel.

    a   List the ways in which they are different from one another.
    b   Make notes on how each of these interpretations differs from the novel.
    c   Write two or three sentences explaining which version of the ending you prefer and why.
    d   Write a paragraph interpreting each of these endings.

 Find out more about the structure of the novel in Unit 11.

Dickens's other ending

Dickens sent the last chapters of the novel to the printer in the middle of June 1861. He then went to stay with his wealthy aristocratic friend Edward Bulwer-Lytton, a hugely popular crime and historical novelist. Dickens showed his host the last chapters of *Great Expectations*. Bulwer-Lytton read that Bentley Drummle died and Estella married a country doctor. Then one day, two years after Pip's return from working in Cairo:

> I was in England again – in London, and walking along Piccadilly with little Pip [Joe and Biddy's son] – when a servant came running after me to ask would I step back to a lady in a carriage who wished to speak to me. It was a little pony carriage, which the lady was driving; and the lady and I looked sadly enough on one another.
>
> 'I am greatly changed, I know; but I thought you would like to shake hands with Estella too, Pip. Lift up that pretty child and let me kiss it!' (She supposed the child, I think, to be my child.)
>
> I was very glad afterwards to have had the interview; for, in her face and in her voice, and in her touch, she gave me the assurance, that suffering had been stronger than Miss Havisham's teaching, and had given her a heart to understand what my heart used to be.

Bulwer-Lytton told Dickens he did not like this downbeat ending. Dickens discarded it and replaced it with the one we read today.

1 Compare Dickens's two endings. In small groups, discuss the following questions.

    a   Why do you think Bulwer-Lytton rejected the original ending?
    b   Why do you think Dickens took his advice?

2 Write a paragraph explaining the ways in which the two endings are different. You should write about:

    a   the narrative (how are the events and facts different?)
    b   the mood (how are the language and imagery different?)

3 Turn your discussions into a short play script (between one and two pages) that reconstructs the conversation between the two novelists. Look at the following list of arguments for each argument and try to weave them into your dialogue.

Arguments favouring the original ending:

- George Bernard Shaw said the novel 'is too serious a book to be a trivially happy one. Its beginning is unhappy; its middle is unhappy; and the conventional happy ending is an outrage on it.'
- The purpose of the second ending is to please a popular audience, which expects a conventional happy ending.
- In the second ending, Pip gets more than he deserves.
- Estella's character has changed too much in the second ending and she is not recognisable as the Estella in the rest of the novel.
- Life is not neat and tidy, and we do not necessarily achieve our dreams. 'Happily ever after' is not realistic.
- Having great expectations is not a recipe for a successful life.

Arguments favouring the revised ending:

- It continues the imagery of the garden and the mist, and is better written.
- It continues the connection of the past and the present, and Pip and Estella's meetings at Satis House.
- The lovers deserve to be happy because they have suffered deeply; their suffering has changed them so much that they are no longer the same people.
- It is appropriate that Magwitch's daughter finds happiness with Pip.

Remember – at the heart of all good drama is conflict. Don't let Dickens give in too easily – think about why he might want to keep the original ending!

 Watch actors performing a conversation between Dickens and Bulwer-Lytton on Cambridge Elevate.

GETTING IT INTO WRITING

Answer this question about the ending of the novel.

Looking closely at the ending of the novel, write about how Dickens brings Pip and Estella back together. Write about:

- **how Dickens presents their relationship at the end of the novel**
- **how Dickens presents the unequal relationship between Pip and Estella in the novel as a whole.**

Learning checkpoint

How will I know I've done this well?

✔ Show understanding of the characters and the relationship between Pip and Estella.

✔ Show understanding of plot and structure.

✔ Quote extracts from the final chapter as part of interpreting the novel's ending.

✔ Write in a formal, critical style.

✔ Use accurate spelling and clear, well-punctuated sentences.

Complete this assignment on Cambridge Elevate.

'parting is a painful thing.'

Pip: Chapter 59

GETTING FURTHER

Narrative ambiguity

Although many people claim that, in making the change, Dickens gave the novel a conventional happy ending, in fact the revised ending is ambiguous. Pip and Estella meet, reflect and leave holding hands, but does this mean they are destined for a happy future together? Their conversation at the end is about friendship, not love or marriage. Estella says that she is glad to be saying goodbye to Pip in Satis House:

'I little thought […] that I should take leave of you in taking leave of this spot. I am very glad to do so.'

Pip protests and says '**parting is a painful thing**', but Estella argues that they will be friends. Their movements are written almost as stage directions:

'We are friends,' said I, rising and bending over her, as she rose from the bench.

1 What do you think?

    a Is Pip's agreement to being friends too enthusiastic for Estella?

    b Is she trying to move further away from him?

    c Estella then says they will be friends '**apart**': is she trying to cool things down?

 Contexts

We know that *Great Expectations* has some autobiographical elements, so perhaps Dickens's own life affected his decision about the ending of the novel. In 1855, when his marriage was collapsing, Dickens was excited to receive a letter from a woman, Maria Beadnell, who he had loved as a young man, but whom he had not seen for 20 years. Arguably, Dickens had used his first meeting with Maria (renamed Dora) in his most autobiographical novel, *David Copperfield*:

I don't remember who was there, except Dora. I have not the least idea what we had for dinner, besides Dora. My impression is, that I dined off Dora, entirely, and sent away half-a-dozen plates untouched. I sat next to her. I talked to her. She had the most delightful little voice, the gayest little laugh, the pleasantest and most fascinating little ways, that ever led a lost youth into hopeless slavery. She was rather diminutive altogether. So much the more precious, I thought.

Their subsequent reunion was a disappointment and, some years later, this event possibly found its way into anther of Dickens's novels, *Little Dorrit* (where this time Maria could be seen as the character Flora). This description is a lot less flattering:

Flora, always tall, had grown to be very broad too, and short of breath; but that was not much. Flora, whom he had left a lily, had become a peony; but that was not much. Flora, who had seemed enchanting in all she said and thought, was diffuse and silly. That was much. Flora, who had been spoiled and artless long ago, was determined to be spoiled and artless now. That was a fatal blow.

Did Dickens's struggle with the ending reflect his experience that reunions are not always a romantic success? Perhaps we should look again at Estella's declaration: '**I am greatly changed**'.

11

Plot and structure

How does Dickens guide the reader through Pip's journey?

SERIALISATION

Great Expectations was published in a magazine called *All the Year Round* in 36 weekly instalments. Most instalments contained just one chapter, but some of them had two. Dickens began work in the autumn of 1860 and finished in June 1861. The first instalment appeared in December 1860 and the last in August 1861. This meant that he was still writing the book even after the first parts had been published, so the development of the story may well have been influenced by the reaction of his readers to certain **characters** and events.

The narrative had to be structured to keep readers interested so that they would want to buy the next instalment. We can see this in the pattern of plots and subplots, each with its own climax and resolution – as well as some exciting **cliff-hangers**.

Sometimes Dickens made the next instalment follow on directly from the last:

Then I put the fastenings as I had found them, opened the door at which I had entered when I ran home last night, shut it, and ran away for the misty marshes.

[…]

It was a rimy morning, and very damp. I had seen the damp lying on the outside of my little window, as if some goblin has been crying there all night, and using the window for a pocket-handkerchief.

This contains the end of the first published episode (comprising Chapters 1 and 2) and the beginning of the second (Chapters 3 and 4). As you can see, the story does not break off between the two sections.

Dickens took the same approach between the end of the second instalment and the beginning of the third (Chapter 5):

But I ran no farther than the house door, for there I ran head foremost into a party of soldiers with their muskets: one of whom held out a pair of handcuffs to me, saying, 'Here you are, look sharp, come on!'

[…]

The apparition of a file of soldiers ringing down the butt-ends of their loaded muskets on our door-step, caused the dinner-party to rise from table in confusion, and caused Mrs. Joe, re-entering the kitchen empty-handed, to stop short and stare, in her wondering lament of 'Gracious goodness gracious me, what's gone – with the – pie!'

 Key terms

cliff-hanger: the end of an episode or an instalment when something surprising happens, so people will want to find out what happens next.

Having established the main lines of the narrative in those first two instalments, Dickens could then use discontinuity and variety, introducing a new plot, setting or character. Look at the end of the fourth instalment and the beginning of the fifth:

Then, the ends of the torches were flung hissing into the water, and went out, as if it were all over with him.

[…]

My state of mind regarding the pilfering from which I had been so unexpectedly exonerated, did not impel me to frank disclosure; but I hope it had some dregs of good at the bottom of it.

The topic is the same, but Dickens moves the story away from Pip's encounter with Magwitch to his reflections on his own behaviour at the time that the convict is caught. The setting has also changed – from out in the marshes with the soldiers to inside Pip's mind, thinking over the events that have occurred.

The fifth instalment is similarly linked to the sixth, as the story and setting move to Mr Pumblechook's house:

But they twinkled out one by one, without throwing any light on the questions why on earth was I going to play at Miss Havisham's and what on earth was I expected to play at.

[…]

Mr Pumblechook's premises in the High-street of the market town, were of a peppercorny and farinaceous nature, as the premises of a corn-chandler and seedsman should be.

 Watch actors reconstruct some of the key moments from Pip's story on Cambridge Elevate.

It was a rimy morning, and very damp.

Chapter 3

89

A NOVEL IN THREE VOLUMES

After serialisation, the **novel** was published in three volumes:

- **Volume 1** has 19 chapters and covers Pip's childhood. He is innocent and naïve. His upbringing is brutal and many of the adults he comes into contact with are unfriendly.
- **Volume 2** has 20 chapters and covers Pip's time in London. Pip seems to lose his way. He treats people poorly, gets into debt and takes little responsibility for his behaviour.
- **Volume 3** has 20 chapters and covers Pip's time with Magwitch, ending with his reunions with Joe and Biddy, then Estella. He seems older and more mature, and has come to terms with the path his life has taken.

Dickens re-read his own novel *David Copperfield* while he was planning *Great Expectations*. However, the new novel was different from earlier ones. The reader initially sympathises with the main character, then loses sympathy, but regains it at the end. This three-part structure, matching the three-volume format, keeps the readers in suspense about how they will eventually feel about the hero of the story.

BILDUNGSROMAN

The overall structure of *Great Expectations* is that of the *bildungsroman*. The structure follows the shape of Pip's life and development, which seems to come full circle:

- **Character:** we meet him as a young boy, watch him grow into an adult and hear him as an older man reflecting on his past.
- **Setting:** we begin with the marshes, the forge and Satis House, and return to these locations in the final scenes.
- **Themes:** Pip wants to be a gentleman; he goes to London to achieve this; he becomes morally and physically ill and is brought back to the marshes by 'a gentle Christian man'.

DEVELOP AND REVISE

Understanding the effects of serialisation

1 At the end of Chapter 2, the convict has threatened to kill Pip and is waiting for him in the churchyard. Find three more examples of a chapter ending with a cliff-hanger.

2 Dickens said that the novel was tightly planned. Consider these three stages of one subplot:

- Orlick's hatred of Pip at the start of the novel
- The mysterious attack on Mrs Joe
- Orlick's seizure of Pip close to the end.

Find three more examples of plots or storylines that begin early in the novel and are only resolved towards the end.

3 Readers needed to remember characters from week to week, and to become familiar with new ones as they appeared.

a Write notes on three minor characters, explaining how Dickens uses **characterisation** to make them instantly recognisable.
b Are Dickens's minor characters portraits or cartoons?

4 Weekly publication as a serial meant that Dickens had to write to strict deadlines and to a particular number of words each month. Do you think he sometimes fills up chapters just to get to the required word count? Give examples to support your answer.

5 Because the work was being published as Dickens wrote, he could not immediately go back and revise earlier chapters. Give examples of any situations or events that you think he should have rewritten. Explain your objections.

Retelling the story

1 Check where the volume divisions are in the novel. Then write a tweet of 140 characters to summarise each volume.

2 Tell the story of Volume 1 in groups of three like this:

a Stand in a triangle, ABC. A starts to tell the story of *Great Expectations* Volume 1 to B. When C claps their hands, B takes over. When C claps their hands again, A takes over and so on. Carry on until you reach the end of Volume 1. If either A or B gets stuck they can call 'swap' and C has to step in to replace them.

b Change roles and repeat the exercise for Volumes 2 and 3.

3 Do you think that the volume divisions are significant in terms of the story, or do they simply divide it into three sections of roughly equal length?

4 Analyse the way each volume ends: does it end with some kind of major drama and excitement, or a turning point in the story?

Writing practice

1 Use your notes from the previous section to help you answer this question:

Dickens wrote *Great Expectations* as a series of weekly instalments in a periodical magazine. Write about:

- **how Dickens structures the story**
- **how you think the structure was influenced by the publication in weekly instalments.**

Remember to back up your ideas with evidence from the text.

Key terms

bildungsroman: a genre of novels that focus on the development, education or coming-of-age of a main character.

12
Context and setting

What do the settings in the novel contribute to the story?

SETTING

Landscapes

The opening of the **novel** is set among the Thames estuary marshes. Some of the description offers authentic details, such as when Pip notices the alders. Sometimes details seem **symbolic** – the gibbet implies justice and the beacon suggests direction. Even the horizon mentioned twice at the end of Chapter 1 conjures up the idea of a limited view at the start of the novel. Pip's story is one of widening horizons and learning new ways of seeing things.

This description on the first page is an effective scene-setter. Gradually the text focuses in on Pip. He is small, cold and distressed in this unwelcoming environment – we realise immediately that this child is not being properly looked after or protected:

… that the dark flat wilderness beyond the churchyard, intersected with dykes and mounds and gates, with scattered cattle feeding on it, was the marshes; and that the low leaden line beyond was the river; and that the distant savage lair from which the wind was rushing, was the sea; and that the small bundle of shivers growing afraid of it all and beginning to cry, was Pip.

Interiors

The homes, inns and places of work in *Great Expectations* are also portrayed in vivid detail. They are rich in implications for the reader to interpret. When Pip looks around Mr Pumblechook's shop, for example, he describes many things that a Victorian reader would expect to see in a corn-chandler's shop, but the store also tells us something about its owner:

It appeared to me that he must be a very happy man indeed, to have so many little drawers in his shop; and I wondered when I peeped into one or two on the lower tiers, and saw the tied-up brown paper packets inside, whether the flower-seeds and bulbs ever wanted of a fine day to break out of those jails, and bloom.

Dickens convincingly describes the neglect that characterises Satis House. It is clearly a place that is not cleaned or looked after properly. However, its cobwebs and dust are also symbolic of its owner, Miss Havisham, who is in a state of sorrow and decay. What do the details in this description suggest about the house? Notice the repetition of **'bars … barred … barred'**:

Within a quarter of an hour we came to Miss Havisham's house, which was of old brick, and dismal, and had a great many iron bars to it. Some of the windows had been walled up; of those that remained, all the lower were rustily barred. There was a courtyard in front, and that was barred.

CONTEXT

Britain in the early 19th century

The main part of *Great Expectations* is set in the second quarter of the 19th century, when Britain was still in the grip of the Industrial Revolution. Many new industries had been established and thousands of people were moving from the countryside to the towns and cities in search of work in factories.

During Dickens's lifetime, the population of Britain more than doubled from 12 million to 25 million. This, along with the sudden growth of towns, created terrible housing conditions and allowed disease to spread rapidly. There was a big gap between the richest and the poorest in society, and the law courts could punish criminals cruelly. Over time, Parliament passed laws reforming society, the economy and the political process to address these issues.

Social justice

As a well-known writer, Dickens's views were influential. Among the **themes** of his novels, he often included issues of social justice:

- treatment of children: education, child labour and child cruelty
- treatment of the poor: poverty, housing conditions, ill-health
- social change: the class system, industrialisation, crime and punishment

Several of these feature in *Great Expectations*.

Education

The young Pip wants to read and write, and he goes to a school in the village run by an elderly shopkeeper, Wopsle's aunt. He only learns anything because one of the older pupils, Biddy, helps him. Joe and Pip's conversation in Chapter 7 shows us that Pip can barely write, while Joe is illiterate.

Child labour

Great Expectations is not about child labour, although Pip does work as a small child. He helps in the forge, and is paid by neighbours to keep birds off crops and collect the stones in fields.

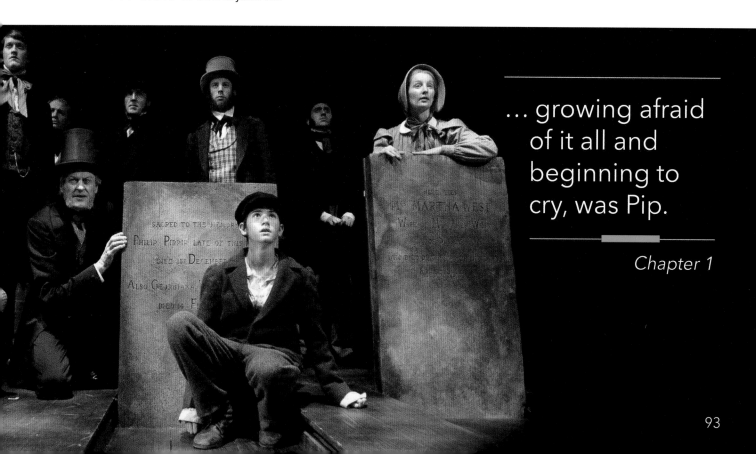

... growing afraid of it all and beginning to cry, was Pip.

Chapter 1

Child cruelty

Pip is treated harshly by his sister. Other adults, such as Pumblechook, treat him without care or respect. Mrs Joe and Pumblechook see Pip's visits to Satis House as an opportunity to make money through him. At the same time, Estella is emotionally abused by Miss Havisham – brought up to be cold and emotionless, and to break men's hearts. Has she overcome this by the end of the novel?

Poverty

As a blacksmith, Joe is skilled at making tools and objects out of metal. The soldiers come to him to mend some shackles when hunting Magwitch. Joe would have shod (put shoes on) horses, which were the main method of transport before railways, tractors, lorries and cars. He is sober and hard-working, and the feast in Chapter 4 suggests that he, Mrs Joe and Pip do not live in fear of hunger. However, Chapter 2 tells us that their house was wooden, so they are clearly not very well-off. What does the description of Joe's and Pip's best clothes in Chapter 4 suggest?

The class system

Pip's journey from an apprentice blacksmith to a gentleman leaves him unsure about who he really is and in search of his true identity. By contrast, Joe – who stays within his class – finds contentment in his work and happiness with Biddy. Dickens is critical of the snobbishness and cruelty of Bentley Drummle. He clearly condemns the injustice that Magwitch suffers at the hand of a system that favours Compeyson. What do you think Dickens's attitude to class is?

Crime and punishment

Prisons were so overcrowded at this time that the government had to use old warships ('hulks') to house prisoners. These were often leaky and in terrible condition. However, they were a cheap and easy way to overcome the problem of prison overcrowding. Magwitch has escaped from one of these, a 'hulk'. What does the story of Molly tell you about the criminal justice system at that time?

DEVELOP AND REVISE

Understanding the meaning of settings and landscapes

1 Copy the table opposite and add to it. When you have finished, discuss the ideas and answers as a group.

Writing about setting

1 Use your text lasso to choose an extract of about 300 words. You could use the **settings** table to help you choose a key quotation. Answer the following question under timed conditions (you will have approximately 50 minutes in the exam). Use the planning method that you developed in Unit 2 and remember to back up your writing with evidence from the text.

Setting is extremely important in *Great Expectations*. Choose one setting from the novel, and write about how Dickens links character and mood to this setting. Write about:

- how Dickens presents mood and character in this extract
- how Dickens uses different settings in the novel as a whole to help the reader understand character and mood.

Setting	Events	Chapter	Quotation	How is the setting used
graveyard on the marshes	convict seizes Pip	1	'and that the dark flat wilderness beyond the churchyard, intersected with dykes and mounds and gates, with scattered cattle feeding on it, was the marshes.'	sinister; menace; danger; uncertainty
forge	childhood home	2	I raised the latch of the door and peeped in at him opposite to it, sitting in the chimney corner. 'Mrs Joe has been out a dozen times, looking for you, Pip … and what's worse, she's got Tickler with her.'	place of security because it is associated with Joe, but also Pip suffers cruelty from his sister who brings him up 'by hand'
Satis House	Pip goes to 'play' and meets Estella, who treats him cruelly	8		
Mr Jaggers's office		20	'Mr Jaggers' room was lighted by a skylight only, and was a most dismal place; the skylight, eccentrically patched like a broken head, and the distorted adjoining houses looking as if they had twisted themselves to peep down at me through it.'	
Wemmick's house	comic **interlude** – Pip visits Wemmick	25		
Thames	attempted escape			
prison				a grim place for Magwitch to die – emphasises the sadness of Magwitch's story, but also shows how devoted Pip is because he continues to visit Magwitch here
ruins of Satis House		59		

Character and characterisation

How does Dickens create such dramatic characters?

DRAWING CHARACTERS

Dickens's observation of people and their trades helped him to write realistic accounts of characters as different as a country blacksmith, a London legal clerk, a convict, a man who lives by recycling clothes from corpses found in the river, and a woman who never recovered from being jilted on her wedding day. Both major and minor characters in the novel are presented with convincing details of how they speak, how they move and what they do.

Speech

Dickens had a very good ear for the way speech reflected personality and culture. Joe Gargery's slow speech is conveyed by his simple phrases. Look at this extract and note the repeated phrases:

'She sot down,' said Joe, 'and she got up, and she made a grab at Tickler, and she Ram-paged out. That's what she did… she Ram-paged out.'

Mrs Joe's speech is constructed to emphasise her speed and abruptness of manner. She uses questions, commands and threats:

'Where have you been, you young monkey?' said Mrs. Joe, stamping her foot. 'Tell me directly what you've been doing to wear me away with fret and fright and worrit, or I'd have you out of that corner if you was fifty Pips, and he was five hundred Gargerys.'

Their actions when speaking also tell us a lot about them. Joe is steady, calm and resigned.

While speaking he is 'slowly clearing the fire between the lower bars with the poker, and looking at it'. Mrs Joe expresses restlessness, barely controlled violence and frustration by 'stamping her foot'.

Behaviour

Dickens creates a strong sense of individual personality through his descriptions of characters' behaviour. For example Orlick's laziness and untidiness is conveyed by repeated use of words such as 'slouching', 'loosely' and 'dangling':

[He] would come slouching from his hermitage, with his hands in his pockets and his dinner loosely tied in a bundle round his neck and dangling on his back. On Sundays he mostly lay all day on the sluice-gates, or stood against ricks and barns.

Mrs Joe's energy is conveyed by Dickens's description of her cutting of a slice of bread:

My sister had a trenchant way of cutting our bread-and-butter for us, that never varied.

The fact that it 'never varied' tells us that this is a mechanical activity, while 'jammed' has a roughness to it.

Read through the rest of the description of Mrs Joe cutting bread. What other language features remind you of machinery, labouring or professional work? What do you think this episode suggests about Mrs Joe's attitude to her role in the home?

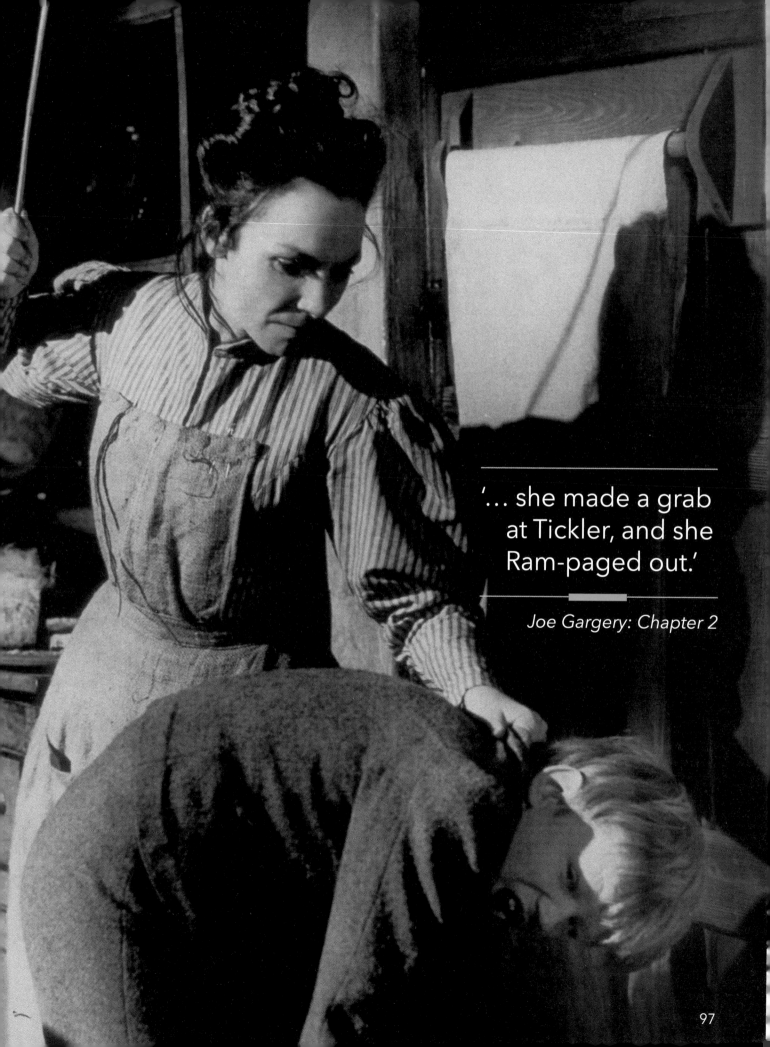

'… she made a grab
at Tickler, and she
Ram-paged out.'

Joe Gargery: Chapter 2

CONNECTING CHARACTERS

Relationships

There are many complex connections between the different characters in the story. Sometimes the links are hidden until late in the novel. For example we do not learn that Estella is related to Molly and Magwitch until near the end. Here are some other connections:

Magwitch used to work with → **Compeyson** who deceived → **Miss Havisham**

Jaggers employs → **Molly** who is → **Estella**'s mother

Estella's father is → **Magwitch** who is → **Pip**'s patron

Pip learns to read from → **Biddy** who later marries → **Joe**

Mrs Joe is killed by → **Orlick** who also works with → **Compeyson** to try and kill → **Magwitch** and **Pip**

Herbert Pocket fights → **Pip** who later studies with Herbert's father → **Matthew Pocket**

DEVELOP AND REVISE

Character sketches

1 Look at the following sketches of each of the major characters in *Great Expectations*. For each statement, find evidence in the novel (an example or a quotation).

> **Pip** begins the novel as a young orphan who knows little of the world. He is treated harshly by his sister but kindly by his brother-in-law. He falls childishly in love with Estella. In London he learns to behave like a gentleman and grows embarrassed by his origins. He continues to be infatuated with Estella, but she remains cold towards him. After the shock of his patron's arrival, he is loyal to Magwitch. Pip rewards Herbert Pocket's friendship by setting him up in business, becoming Herbert's secret benefactor, as Magwitch was his. He meets Estella 11 years later and seems confident they will now never part.

Estella is beautiful – this is what Pip tells us both as a character (when a child) and as narrator. She mocks him and slaps him. Miss Havisham is training her to break men's hearts. She seems emotionally challenged and incapable of love as a result. It is hard to be sure whether, as an adult, she treats Pip with unkindness or indifference, whether she is cruel or unable to understand his feelings. By the end of the novel she has suffered herself, and seems to have developed a wider range of emotions, but her communication is restrained and her feelings for Pip remain ambiguous.

Abel Magwitch is a fearsome convict who threatens to murder a young boy. As he eats the pie Pip brings him, we understand that his behaviour is driven by desperation. His confession that he stole the pie (to protect Pip) shows an underlying decency. The revelation that he worked to earn a fortune and spend it on Pip raises many questions. Is he trying to father Pip, having lost his own daughter? Is he trying to make up for his treatment of Pip that day? Or reward him for his help? Is he trying to live his life again through Pip?

Miss Havisham is cruel. Her cruelty stems from being deceived by Compeyson, who took her money and then did not marry her. She has never recovered from this and sees all men as enemies to punish. Estella is the tool she uses to do this. She teaches Estella to break men's hearts. Inviting Pip to play is part of Estella's training. Just before her death, she understands what she has done and begs for forgiveness.

Joe Gargery is a simple man and a loyal friend to Pip. His speech is often comically confused, but he shows wisdom and understanding. He does not stand in Pip's way when opportunity knocks, and allows him to go to London even though he will be lonely without Pip. He is the one person who remains at Pip's bedside during his illness. His character grows and develops throughout the novel. At the end, we know he will be a good husband to Biddy.

Herbert Pocket fights Pip bravely and correctly at the start of the novel. He shows no hard feelings at the end of the bout, revealing his upbeat and cheerful nature. When Pip meets him in London, he becomes a good friend and willingly teaches Pip the manners of a gentleman. Herbert readily agrees to take part in the dangerous plans for Magwitch's escape. He achieves success in love and (with Pip's help) in work.

Mr Jaggers hides behind his cold and calculated lawyer's language. We rarely know what he is thinking or feeling. He keeps secrets: Pip's benefactor's identity; the fact that Molly is Estella's mother. Towards the end of the novel, Jaggers explains why he arranged for Estella to be adopted by Miss Havisham. Has he a concealed human caring side, as his clerk Wemmick does?

Connecting people

1 Create a spider diagram showing the different relationships in the novel. You can use the following example as a starting point.

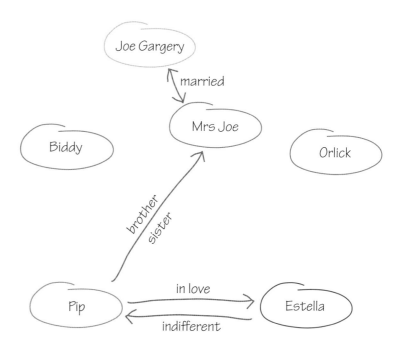

14

Themes and ideas

What are the big themes and ideas that dominate *Great Expectations*?

RECURRING THEMES

Country and city

Dickens's opening descriptions of the countryside present it as flat, cold and threatening. The village Pip leaves in Chapter 19 is '**peaceful and quiet**'. His London is a marked contrast. When Pip first arrives, he goes sightseeing. He visits Smithfield market (a symbol of trade), the Old Bailey (a symbol of justice) and St Paul's Cathedral (a symbol of religious faith). Dickens records Pip's reactions as:

- disgust at the '**filth and fat and blood and foam**' of Smithfield's
- horror at being invited by a drunken legal officer to see criminals being sentenced to death at the Old Bailey
- alarm when St Paul's '**Bulged at me**', like some active and menacing force.

Parenting

Dickens often wrote about growing up, and especially about the way adults affect children's lives. In *Great Expectations*, Joe is always kind and gentle, and he treats Pip as an equal. He tries to protect Pip and comfort him with extra helpings of gravy and a bread-eating competition. At the end of the novel, he carries Pip, like a loving father, back to the forge.

Mrs Joe, who has no children of her own, beats her small brother and continually criticises him, complaining about the burden he has been.

Mrs Pocket has so many children that she is never sure where they all are. She depends on a nursemaid to do the actual work of childcare. Dickens suggests the lack of care in parenting by describing her children as '**tumbling up**' rather than growing up.

Childhood

The humour that Dickens intended for this novel begins on the first page, where Pip imagines what his parents looked like from the lettering on their gravestones. However, this episode is intended to offer insight as well as amusement, and it reveals much about the character of the young Pip and the life he leads.

The Christmas dinner episode in Chapter 2 is another mixture of humour and insight. The adults lecture Pip and ignore him by turns. The neglect is expressed through comedy: while they over-eat, he is left with '**those obscure corners of pork of which the pig, when alive, had the least reason to be vain**'. The good-natured Joe – who cannot express his sympathy in words – tries to console Pip with gravy.

Magwitch recalls the contrast between how he saw himself as a child and how others saw him:

'… when I was a ragged little creetur as much to be pitied as ever I see […] I got the name of being hardened. "This is a terrible hardened one," they says to prison wisitors, picking out me. "May be said to live in jails, this boy."'

Doctors measure him, believing that they can assess his criminality in this way, while Christian prison visitors preach to him about good and evil. None of them takes care of him, so he is forced to take care of himself. The contrast between well-fed adult absurdity and a child who is physically and emotionally hungry is reflected in Pip's childhood.

Justice

Dickens knew about the justice system from childhood and his experiences as a journalist. Jaggers makes a living out of representing those who can afford to pay. Wemmick supplements his income by acquiring '**portable property**' from those who are soon to be executed.

Magwitch's story involves prison ships, transportation and Newgate Prison. Like the description of the landscape with which the book begins, the account of his trial and death sentence is more than scenery:

The sun was striking in at the great windows of the court, through the glittering drops of rain upon the glass, and it made a broad shaft of light between the two-and-thirty and the Judge, linking both together, and perhaps reminding some among the audience how both were passing on, with absolute equality, to the greater Judgment that knoweth all things, and cannot err.

The **theme** of justice goes beyond Magwitch. Mrs Joe describes Pip in criminal terms, accusing him of '**acts of sleeplessness**' and illnesses he had been '**guilty**' of, thus connecting him to the convict and the theme.

Escape

Escaping one's circumstances is an important theme in the novel. Pip escapes his poor education and the work of the forge. Mr Wopsle escapes his humble life in the village to become an actor in London. Wemmick escapes from the grim realities of his work in prisons to his castle in the country. Magwitch escapes imprisonment and exile, but is captured again both times. Miss Havisham does not escape her past – she chooses to live in it.

Class

Pip's 'expectations' are the fortune he believes he will inherit, but also the ambitions he has harboured since he was a child. Becoming a gentleman begins with a change of clothes and proceeds to a change of manners. Herbert Pocket, the son of a gentleman, acts as Pip's mentor, instructing him in the social skills expected of him.

Herbert's own family, though well connected, is short of money and accordingly has young men come to board. One of these, Bentley Drummle, courts Estella. He is richer than Herbert, but has none of the same attractive qualities. He has more social skills than Pip, but none of his human qualities.

Love

Miss Havisham's disappointment in love has made her bitter and vengeful. She uses Estella as a way of getting her revenge on men. Estella herself is ruined by this upbringing, growing arrogant and cruel, making Pip feel inadequate and inferior, even when they are children.

Biddy maintains a secret love for Pip and is hurt by his love for the undeserving Estella. However, Biddy later finds true love and happiness with Joe.

Joe is the constant source of love and stability for the young Pip. He symbolically takes him back to the forge to begin his re-growth after the death of Magwitch.

Wemmick shows his tender side in his love for his aging father and his affection for Miss Skiffins.

How we understand the end of the novel, where Pip and Estella meet again, depends on whether we believe they are capable of true love and commitment to each other.

Wealth

Pip believes that the money that turns him into a gentleman comes from Miss Havisham. His shock at discovering that Magwitch is his benefactor is similar to his embarrassment when Joe comes to visit him in London. Pip's wealth has made him focus on people's social class and manners, overlooking their moral worth and their care for him.

DEVELOP AND REVISE

What's in a name?

Characters, places and events can suggest more than one theme, and similar themes and ideas might be called different things. For example the ideas explored in 'country and city' might equally be applied under 'landscapes', 'settings' or 'descriptions'. The ideas in 'justice' could be discussed as 'crime and punishment', and so on.

1 Which ideas might recur in a discussion of:

    a ambition and self-improvement
    b society
    c men and women
    d virtue and good character
    e self-knowledge and identity
    f love, loyalty and deceit?

Turning abstract to concrete

Because themes and ideas are abstract, it can be difficult to make notes on them, build up your knowledge and then revise. It can help to connect them with something concrete and specific.

1 Draw up a table showing where different themes occur in the novel, and the people and places with which they are associated. Use the following table as a starting point. Add as many rows as you can.

Miss Havisham was going to make my fortune on a grand scale.

Chapter 18

Theme(s)	Character(s)	Place	Event	Quotation	How this refers to the theme
ambition and self-improvement; social class	Pip; Mr Jaggers	the forge	Mr Jaggers tells Pip that he has a secret benefactor who wants him to become a gentleman and will fund him to do this.	'My dream was out; my wild fancy was surpassed by sober reality; Miss Havisham was going to make my fortune on a grand scale.'	Pip seizes on this chance to better himself – he does not realise there will be losses as well as gains.
ambition and self-improvement; social class				'So imperfect was this realisation of the first of my great expectations …'	
			Herbert gives Pip a lesson in table manners.		
			Joe visits Pip in London.		

15

Language

Why does the language in *Great Expectations* have such an impact?

DIFFERENT TYPES OF LANGUAGE

Everything Dickens does in *Great Expectations* is done through language. **Dialogue**, narrative, **characterisation**, **settings**, ideas and moods are all communicated through his choice of words. In Unit 13 you investigated how speech builds **character** and how the dialogue is similar to that in a play or a film – well suited to being read aloud. The characters are given dramatically interesting speech habits that an actor can bring to life.

Narrative and setting

Dickens conveys a sense of the movement of the Thames and the docklands with a remarkable 164-word sentence early in Chapter 54. This sentence shows his knowledge of nautical business, listing items out on the river:

… rusty chain-cables … frayed hempen hawsers … bobbing buoys … floating broken baskets … floating chips of wood and shaving … scum of coal.

It is also full of activity and energy demonstrated through 'ing' verbs: 'avoiding', 'bobbing', 'sinking', 'floating', 'scattering', 'shaving', 'cleaving', 'making', 'starting', 'clashing', 'roaring' and 'fishing'. Some of these are repeated - 'going' occurs six times:

… hammers going in ship-builders' yards, saws going at timber, clashing engines going at things unknown, pumps going in leaky ships, capstans going, ships going out to sea …

This flowing sentence matching the flowing river, its purpose is to show the business of the Thames. However, if you look at the narrative **context** you realise that this describes the departure of a small boat carrying the escaping Magwitch. In all this detail, their boat is one small action among many. This is like a film shot following an individual in a busy crowd of people.

Dialogue

In Chapter 2, Dickens combines the comedy of Joe's concern for Pip's well-being with Pip's own concern to hide food so that he can take it to Magwitch. Dickens uses language to convey Joe's slow movements and equally slow thought processes. The sentences make the simple activity of eating bread seem like something requiring thought and effort:

He turned it about in his mouth much longer than usual, pondering over it a good deal, and after all gulped it down like a pill.

Dickens shows how slowly Joe speaks by creating large pauses, interrupting with descriptions of Joe's actions:

'You know, Pip,' said Joe, solemnly, with his last bite in his cheek, and speaking in a confidential voice, as if we two were quite alone, 'you and me is always friends.'

Dickens similarly slows down his next speech with another 'stage direction':

… said Joe, looking at me, and not at Mrs. Joe, with his bite still in his cheek …

Vocabulary

When Pip encounters Trabb's boy, who mocks his return to the village in smart clothes, Pip's narrative language is formal. He is trying to be dignified and superior:

Casting my eyes along the street at a certain point of my progress, I beheld Trabb's boy approaching, lashing himself with an empty blue bag. Deeming that a serene and unconscious contemplation of him would best beseem me, and would be most likely to quell his evil mind, I advanced with that expression of countenance, and was rather congratulating myself on my success …

Notice the vocabulary: '**progress**', '**serene**', '**unconscious**', '**contemplation**', '**beseem**', '**quell**', '**advanced**', '**countenance**', '**congratulating**'. These words are intended to show the education that Pip (as **narrator**) has subsequently received.

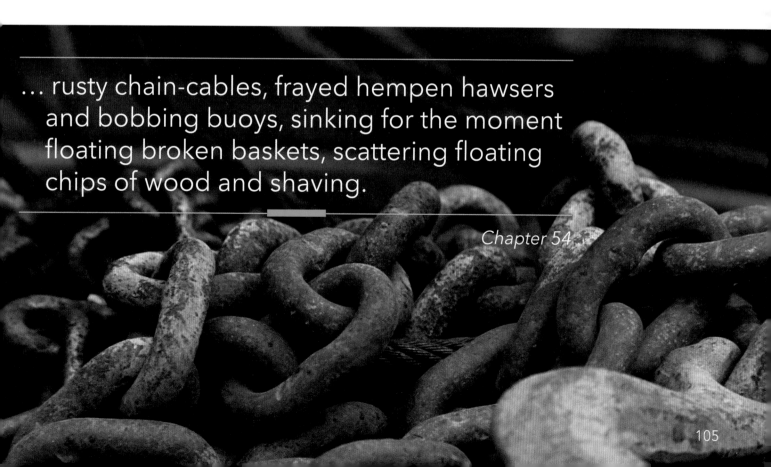

… rusty chain-cables, frayed hempen hawsers and bobbing buoys, sinking for the moment floating broken baskets, scattering floating chips of wood and shaving.

Chapter 54

LANGUAGE CHANGES

Dickens wrote *Great Expectations* more than 150 years ago. The English language and attitudes towards language have changed in this time:

- Words come into and go out of fashion.
- New technology means new words are invented.
- As old technology stops being used, some words fall out of use.
- Attitudes about language change.

When reading the **novel**, and in particular when writing about it, consider how any old-fashioned words or language contribute to mood and characterisation.

 Watch an interview about language on Cambridge Elevate.

DEVELOP AND REVISE

Hidden meanings

Look at the following extract from the novel and the annotations about the information hidden in the language:

She doesn't use his name (sees him as a boy not a person).

This is more formal, adult language. It uses the first person and is the voice of an adult looking back.

Suggests that the only important thing about them is the way they look – but hands and shoes are far more important for what they do!

Goes with 'accessories' – suggests these are extra and not important.

'You are to wait here, you boy,' said Estella; and disappeared and closed the door.

I took the opportunity of being alone in the court-yard to look at my coarse hands and my common boots. My opinion of those accessories was not favourable. They had never troubled me before, but they troubled me now, as vulgar appendages. I determined to ask Joe why he had ever taught me to call those picture-cards, Jacks, which ought to be called knaves. I wished Joe had been rather more genteelly brought up, and then I should have been so too.

He sees himself through her eyes, and she has made him ashamed of himself.

'coarse', 'common', 'vulgar appendages': he uses Estella's higher-class language to criticise himself.

He blames Joe for the way he has been brought up.

Both classes play cards – it's only what you call them that makes you 'genteel' or 'vulgar'.

Contrast: 'genteel' is socially superior to vulgar'.

1 Look at the following extract from Chapter 20, where Pip describes a part of the carriage in which he travels:

His getting on his box, which I remember to have been decorated with an old weather-stained pea-green hammercloth moth-eaten into rags, was quite a work of time. It was a wonderful equipage, with six great coronets outside, and ragged things behind for I don't know how many footmen to hold on by, and a harrow below them, to prevent amateur footmen from yielding to the temptation.

Using the annotated extract as a model, write annotations for the following words and phrases:

a   weather-stained
b   hammercloth
c   moth-eaten into rags
d   quite a work of time
e   equipage
f   coronets
g   amateur footmen.

 Watch a discussion about this activity on Cambridge Elevate.

Writing about language

1 Look at this extract from Chapter 27:

'Which you have that growed,' said Joe, 'and that swelled, and that gentle-folked,' Joe considered a little before he discovered this word; 'as to be sure you are a honour to your king and country.'
'And you, Joe, look wonderfully well.'

Comment on how Dickens uses language to

a   characterise and contrast Joe and Pip
b   dramatise the ideas of class, growing up and education.

2 Choose a 300-word extract that includes one of the short passages analysed in this unit. Write a short essay commenting on:

a   plot (what is happening?)
b   character (who are these people and what are we finding out about them?)
c   **themes** (what ideas are being dramatised here?)
d   language (what is Dickens doing with words and why is he doing it?)

Preparing for your exam

You progress in this section:

- understand what the exam requires and the skills you need to show
- prepare for your exam by planning and responding to a practice question
- assess your skills against example responses to the question
- improve your skills in writing for GCSE English Literature.

What the exam requires

For your GCSE English Literature, you will be assessed on *Great Expectations* in Section A of **Paper 1: Shakespeare and the 19th-century novel**. You will have 1 hour and 45 minutes to complete Paper 1 and it is worth 40% of your GCSE English Literature.

You will have to answer one question on *Great Expectations*. You will be required to write in detail about an extract from the novel that is printed in your exam paper, and then to write about the novel as a whole. The question is worth 30 marks.

The assessment objective skills

Your answers will be assessed against three assessment objectives (AOs) – skills that you are expected to show. These are shown in full in the introductory section and outlined below in relationship to your responses. Notice the marks for each assessment objective and take account of this as you manage your time and focus your response.

- **AO1:** Read, understand and write about what happens in the novel, referring to the text and using relevant quotations (12 marks).
- **AO2:** Analyse the language, form and structure used by Dickens to create meanings and effects (12 marks).
- **AO3:** Show an understanding of the context of the novel. This might include, depending on the question, when Dickens wrote the novel, the period in which he set the novel and why it was set then, its relevance to readers then and to you in the 21st century (6 marks).

What to do in the exam

- At the beginning of the exam, spend some time looking very carefully at the question. Make sure you understand exactly what you are being asked to do.
- Annotate the extract and plan what you want to write about for the extract and the novel as a whole.

Read the practice question and the annotations.

Dialogue: she doesn't use his name (sees him as a boy not a person).

'You are to wait here, you boy,' said Estella; and disappeared and closed the door.

I took the opportunity of being alone in the court-yard to look at my coarse hands and my common boots. My opinion of those accessories was not favourable. They had never troubled me before, but they troubled me now, as vulgar appendages. I determined to ask Joe why he had ever taught me to call those picture-cards, Jacks, which ought to be called knaves. I wished Joe had been rather more genteelly brought up, and then I should have been so too.

She came back, with some bread and meat and a little mug of beer. She put the mug down on the stones of the yard, and gave me the bread and meat without looking at me, as insolently as if I were a dog in disgrace. I was so humiliated, hurt, spurned, offended, angry, sorry – I cannot hit upon the right name for the smart – God knows what its name was – that tears started to my eyes. The moment they sprang there, the girl looked at me with a quick delight in having been the cause of them. This gave me power to keep them back and to look at her: so, she gave a contemptuous toss – but with a sense, I thought, of having made too sure that I was so wounded – and left me.

But, when she was gone, I looked about me for a place to hide my face in, and got behind one of the gates in the brewery-lane, and leaned my sleeve against the wall there, and leaned my forehead on it and cried. As I cried, I kicked the wall, and took a hard twist as my hair; so bitter were my feelings, and so sharp was the smart without a name, that needed counteraction.

Narrative: she has made him ashamed of being coarse and common, unlike her.

Word choice: goes with 'coarse' and 'common'. Blames Joe for the way he has brought him up.

Contrast: 'genteel' is socially superior to 'vulgar'.

Comparison: even when doing him a favour, she makes it seem that he is inferior, like a dog. All this is very painful to him.

She is pleased to see that she has hurt him.

Detail of child-like behaviour.

He seems to be punishing himself.

This event makes a strong impression on him and the way he grows up later in the novel.

Start with a close reference to the text, on the printed extract, before widening your response to the novel as a whole. (AO1, AO2)

This asks you to include contextual elements. In this case, the topic is unequal relationships. You need to stick to this. (AO3)

Starting with this extract, write about how Dickens presents the unequal relationship between Pip and Estella. Write about:

- how Dickens presents Pip's feelings in this extract
- how Dickens presents the unequal relationship between Pip and Estella in the novel as a whole.

[30 marks]

The bullet points remind you to focus on both the extract and the novel as a whole.

Plan your answer

When planning your answer to any question, you should focus on three key areas:

- What do you know about the characters, events and ideas at this stage – in this extract and in the novel as a whole? (AO1)
- What comments can you make about how Dickens uses language and style, using examples from this extract? (AO2)
- What is relevant in this extract that relates to the context of the novel as a whole? (AO3)

Look at this example of a student's plan. Then explore the example paragraphs and development of skills in writing for GCSE English Literature that follow.

Estella's first words and Pip's reaction

Estella's manner and effects on Pip

Pip's feelings about his hands and boots

Estella's mocking of Pip's language and his feelings about Joe

Pip hiding his feelings from Estella and expressing them when she has gone

Estella's motives and effects on Pip from now on

Estella and Pip at Satis House following the first meeting

Estella and Pip as they grow up

Estella and Pip after Magwitch's capture and trial

Estella and Pip in the alternative endings

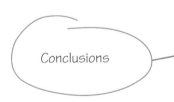
Conclusions

- How Dickens presents Pip's feelings in this extract .
- How Dickens presents the unequal relationship between Pip and Estella in the novel as a whole.

Remember:

✔ **The best answers** will explore Dickens's craft and purpose in creating characters and relationships. They will connect what the characters and relationships do, to the writer's ideas and to the effects upon a reader. They offer a personal response and many well-explained details.

✔ **Good answers** will show a clear understanding of how Dickens develops the characters and the relationship between Pip and Estella, using well-chosen examples.

✔ **Weaker answers** will only explain what happens to characters and the relationship between Pip and Estella, without using many examples or mentioning how Dickens presents them.

Show your skills

To help you think about your own writing, look at these six example paragraphs of writing about *Great Expectations*. The annotations show the range of skills displayed in each paragraph.

Pip is an orphan who is being brought up by his sister and her husband, Joe Gargery the blacksmith. This is the first time he meets Estella, who makes him feel very low class.

> some simple facts stated

When Pip goes to Miss Havisham's, Estella comments rudely on his 'coarse' hands and 'common' boots, and mocks him for calling the Knave cards 'Jacks'.

> statement supported with quotation

Dickens has presented Pip so far as a working boy in Joe's forge, and this is his first meeting with someone who treats him as if he is low class, with 'vulgar appendages'. Dickens makes the reader sympathise with Pip when Estella mocks his hands, clothes and speech and makes him feel ashamed of himself. This makes him want to improve himself, which is what happens later in the novel.

> explanation structured by reference to author, reader and other parts of the text

Dickens makes Pip feel humiliated by Estella's mockery of his appearance ('coarse' hands and 'common' boots) and his language (calling the Knaves 'Jacks'). He has not met people of Estella's class and education before, and now feels ashamed that Joe has not brought him up 'genteelly'. He doesn't want to show her that he is hurt so he took out his frustration by kicking the wall and twisting his hair.

> provides a range of details to keep clearly illustrating a point

Pip's first meeting with Estella conveys the idea of different classes, with Pip being the low-class 'vulgar' person with 'coarse hands' and 'common boots'. Dickens shows Estella's cruel, arrogant behaviour as the result of Miss Havisham using Estella to get her revenge on men. In a way, Miss Havisham has a bad effect on Pip and on Estella, making both of them victims of her own bitterness.

> uses details to develop an interpretation going beyond what the text states explicitly

Pip's first meeting with Estella brings in the idea of social class differences because it is the first time that Pip thinks of himself as lower class, with 'coarse hands' and 'common boots'. This has a strong psychological effect on him, because it makes him think Joe is to blame for his 'vulgar appendages' and not bringing him up 'genteelly'. This is part of Dickens's comment on social divisions in the 19th century, but to some extent people today can still feel inferior if people mock their clothes or their speech. The feeling of being inferior that Estella causes Pip makes him determined to be a gentleman later on, and makes him feel uncomfortable when he is with Joe.

> an argued interpretation focused on author, contexts and ideas

Plan and write your own response

Now plan and write your own response to the practice question.
You can then assess your skills against the example responses that follow.

 Complete this assignment on Cambridge Elevate.

ASSESS YOUR SKILLS

The following extracts are from sample responses to the practice question. They provide examples of skills at different levels when writing for GCSE English Literature.

Use these examples to assess your own skills in responding to the practice question, so that you know what you do well and can focus on areas to improve. Compare the extracts with your own answer to the exam practice question. As you read the responses, think about how far each example – and your own answer – is successful in:

- sustaining focus on the question
- supporting comment with textual detail
- making use of textual detail to build interpretation
- linking detail with Dickens's craft in writing a novel and his purpose in conveying characters, relationships and ideas.

Student A

This is taken from early in Student A's response:

Pip is a young orphan boy who lives with his blacksmith adopted parent Joe Gargery and his wife, Mrs Joe. He has no friends and only adults around him so he is lonely. He gets told he has to visit Miss Havisham, who lives in a big posh house called Satis House in the village, which makes him a bit nervous. When Pip goes to Miss Havisham's, Estella, who lives with her, is rude about his 'coarse' hands and 'common' boots.

This is taken from further on in Student A's response:

Later on, Pip realises that Estella is not what she seemed. He thought she was a posh young lady, but her real mother Molly was very poor and had 20 years of a brutal husband and a stormy life before giving her to Miss Havisham to look after. This is a bit like Pip, who thought that someone posh had left him his money, but it turned out to be the convict. Magwitch turned out to be Estella's father and this brings them together, after a long while, at the end of the book, showing that they were more equal than they seemed to be at first.

In these parts of the response, Student A engages with the character as a real person, rather than the character as a product of the writer's craft. The response shows:

- understanding of character, but not characterisation
- obvious textual detail to support simple comment on character and relationship
- awareness of the character's attitude and feeling
- awareness of the character's development during the course of the novel
- awareness of settings and the effect on the character.

Student B

This is taken from early in Student B's response:

Dickens makes Pip feel put down by Estella's mockery of his 'coarse' hands and 'common' boots and calling the Knaves 'Jacks'. He has not met people of Estella's class and education before, and she makes him feel ashamed of his 'vulgar appendages' and resentful that Joe has not brought him up 'genteelly'. She even makes fun of the way he speaks, because he calls the Knave cards 'Jacks'. Dickens is showing the effects of social class here, which makes Pip feel inferior.

This is taken from further on in Student B's response:

Later on the novel, Pip learns how to be a gentleman, wearing a good suit made by Mr Trabb and learning from Herbert how to manage cutlery at the table. He learns that 'in London it is not the custom to put the knife in the mouth – for fear of accidents – and that while the fork is reserved for that use, it is not put further in than necessary'. This makes him feel embarrassed by Joe's manners when Joe visits him. Estella marries someone she thought was a gentleman but turns out to be a rogue. Eventually, they both find out that they owe a lot to the convict Magwitch, who is Estella's father and Pip's benefactor. Dickens shows that Pip and Estella come to realise that there is more to life than talking in a posh way or coming from a posh family.

This is a stronger response than Student A. In these parts of the response, Student B is clearly focused on the author's craft and purpose. The response engages with character and relationship. It includes personal interpretation. It shows:

- understanding of Dickens's characterisation
- sustained comment on meaning of textual detail
- use and effect of particular word choices e.g. 'coarse', 'common' and 'vulgar' contrasted with 'genteelly'
- some exploration of Estella's feelings and motives
- exploration of characters' development and what they learn
- links between textual detail and author's ideas
- how Pip's attitudes develop and change during the course of the novel
- Pip's relationships with others and how these teach him lessons about the world, in particular Joe and Magwitch.

Student C

This is taken from early in Student C's response:

Dickens presents Pip as a sensitive young boy who is easily hurt. His first meeting with Estella is very hurtful. Estella has been brought up to take revenge on all men because of Miss Havisham's bitter experience of one man, and humiliates Pip through no fault of his own. The meeting with Estella brings in the idea of social class differences because it is the first time that Pip thinks of himself as lower class, with 'coarse hands' and 'common boots'. This has a strong psychological effect on him, because it makes him blame Joe for his 'vulgar appendages' and not bringing him up 'genteelly'. This is part of Dickens's comment on social divisions in the 19th century, but to some extent people today can still feel inferior if others mock their clothes or their speech. The feeling of being inferior that Estella causes Pip makes him determined to be a gentleman later on, and makes him uncomfortable when he is with Joe. The novel is a 'growing up' novel (a 'bildungsroman'), which shows the influence of cultural differences on a person's development.

This is taken from further on in Student C's response:

Dickens develops several of the ideas from this early relationship. Because of Estella's cruel words, Pip becomes determined to make himself a gentleman in his dress and behaviour, but their lives don't work out the way they hoped. Estella enters into a bad marriage with Bentley Drummle, who does not have coarse hands or common boots, and is the next heir but one to a baronetcy, but who is less of a 'gentle man' than Pip. Dickens wrote two endings for the novel, one suggesting that the two of them might get together after all that happened, and the other suggesting that nothing could bring them together. Perhaps Dickens thought the second one more true to life, but he may have thought his readers would prefer the happy ending.

This is the best of the three student responses. In these parts of the response, Student C shows exploration of Dickens's ideas and purposes, with evaluation of the novel's relevance to wider ideas and social and literary contexts. The response shows:

* well-used textual detail to support interpretations
* a grasp of Dickens's crafting of the structure for different effects on the reader
* exploration of writer's ideas
* focus on effect on readers
* how Pip's attitudes develop and change during the course of the novel
* connection of the novel with concepts of social status and class and how they are presented, and contexts then and now
* form and genre comments, such as *bildungsroman*.

Use what you have learned from this section to focus on skills to improve for your examination.

Practice questions

Read the practice question and the annotations.

Use your learning in this section to create practice questions and develop your skills further.

1 Work with another student to:

- choose a topic from the list in this section, or a topic of your choice
- choose a suitable extract of around 300 words
- create your practice question.

Use these prompts to create your question:

- Choose a suitable topic.
- Choose a suitable extract.
- Choose a focus for writing about the extract.

Your question should look like this:

Starting with this extract, write about how Dickens presents your choice of topic. Write about:

- **how Dickens presents your choice of focus in this extract**
- **how Dickens presents your choice of topic as above in this extract.**

Topics

You could choose from the following themes, which Dickens explores in the novel:

- dreams or ambitions
- affections or loyalties
- meanness or generosity
- a major character
- a minor character
- relationships
- a domestic setting
- children and adults.

2 Now answer the question, using the skills you have developed.

As you plan and write, think about how you can:

- sustain your focus on the question
- support comments with textual detail
- make use of textual detail to build interpretation
- link detail with Dickens' craft in writing a novel and his purpose in conveying characters and ideas.

3 Swap work with your partner. Using these points and your work in this section, comment on the skills shown in the answer. Suggest three areas that could be improved.

 Complete this assignment on Cambridge Elevate.

'I have often thought of you,'
said Estella

Chapter 59

Glossary

bildungsroman a genre of novels that focus on the development, education or coming-of-age of a main character

characterisation the way in which writers establish and develop characters by describing features that are unique or distinctive

characters the people in a story; even when based on real people, characters in novels are invented or fictionalised

cliff-hanger the end of an episode or an instalment when something surprising happens, so people will want to find out what happens next

context the historical circumstances of a piece of writing, which affect what an author wrote and the way they wrote it

contrast to point out the ways in which two or more things are different from each other

dialectic an organised discussion between two people who disagree on an issue

dialogue a conversation between two or more people in a piece of writing

first person a way of writing that tells a story through the eyes of one of the characters, using the pronouns 'I', 'my' and 'me'

improvise to make something up as you go along, with no planning

interlude a scene or event that provides a break from the main action of a story

interpretation your understanding of the meaning of what characters say and do

mock-heroic writing in which the style is too formal or dramatic for the subject-matter

narrative tension the excitement the reader feels as they turn the page to find out what happens next in the story

narrator the character in a novel who tells the story in the first person

novel a long story written in prose, describing characters and events

nuance a subtle meaning or shade of meaning that is not always obvious in a text

pathos from the Greek word meaning 'suffering', this is an appeal to the reader's emotions, particularly passages likely to cause pity and sorrow

setting the description of the place in which a novel is set

storyboard a sequence of drawings that show the different scenes in a story or levels in a video game

subtext the unwritten part of a text – the ideas that are hidden beneath the words

symbolism the use of words or images to suggest an idea or emotion

theme an idea that a writer keeps returning to, exploring it from different perspectives

Acknowledgements

Picture credits

cover Remi Cauzid/Shutterstock; p. 5 (t) iStock/
Thinkstock; p. 5 (b) Everett Historical/Shutterstock;
p. 7 AF Archive/Alamy; p. 11 AF Archive/Alamy;
p. 12 RCKeller/Thinkstock; p. 13 Richard_
Lightscapes/Thinkstock; p. 14 Alastair Muir/
Rex Features; p. 15 Moviestore Collection Ltd/
Alamy; p. 18 Classic Image/Alamy; p. 20 Rüdiger
Wittmann/Thinkstock; p. 21 AF Archive/Alamy; p.
23 Moviestore Collection Ltd/Alamy;
p. 25 Pictorial Press Ltd/Alamy; p. 27 Photos.
com/Thinkstock; p. 28 flocu/Thinkstock; p. 29
Pres Panayotov/Shutterstock; p. 31 Geraint Lewis/
Alamy; p. 32 ITV/Rex Features; p. 34 Heritage
Image Partnership Ltd./Alamy; p. 35 Moviestore
Collection Ltd/Alamy; p. 37 Geraint Lewis/Alamy;
p. 39 Donald Cooper/Photostage; p. 42 Andrea
Danti/Thinkstock; p. 43 AF Archive/Alamy; p. 47
Photos 12/Alamy; p. 50 arianarama/Thinkstock;
p. 51 AF Archive/Alamy; p. 55 Geraint Lewis/
Alamy; p. 56 Francis Loney/ArenaPAL/Topfoto;
p. 58 belchonock/Thinkstock; p. 59 macbrianmun/
Thinkstock; p. 60 AF Archive/Alamy; p. 64
johnnorth/Thinkstock; p. 67 RichardBarrow/
Thinkstock; p. 69 AF Archive/Alamy; p. 71 Hulton
Archive/Getty Images; p. 72 Shaiith/Thinkstock;
p. 73 Yanik Chauvin/Thinkstock; p. 75 AF Archive/
Alamy; p. 77 Nigel Norrington/ArenaPAL/Topfoto;
p. 70 AF Archive/Alamy; p. 80 firina/Thinkstock;
p. 81 AF Archive/Alamy; p. 83 aniszewski/
Thinkstock; p. 86 Donald Cooper/Photostage;
p. 88 EddieThomas/Thinkstock; p. 89 catolla/
Thinkstock; p. 92 dundanim/Thinkstock; p. 93
Nigel Norrington/ArenaPAL/Topfoto; p. 96
Geraint Lewis/Alamy; p. 97 Moviestore Collection
Ltd./Alamy; p. 98 Photos.com/Thinkstock;
p. 100 skynetphoto/Thinkstock; p. 103 Sementer/
Thinkstock; p. 104 leungchopan/Thinkstock;
p. 105 Brian Patrick/Thinkstock; p. 108 Pictorial
Press Ltd/Alamy; p. 117 Geraint Lewis/Alamy.

Produced for Cambridge University Press by

 White-Thomson Publishing
www.wtpub.co.uk

Editor: Sonya Newland
Designer: Clare Nicholas